THE
STORY
OF
BASKETBALL

A lavishly illustrated history of the sport from 1891 to today, The Story of Basketball *is primarily a story of people. Its all-star cast includes heroes of the past such as Hank Luisetti, George Mikan, and Bill Russell and heroes of the present such as Kareem Abdul-Jabbar, Rick Barry, and Julius Erving. It's also the story of such great teams as the Minneapolis Lakers of the 1950s, the Boston Celtics of the '60s, and the UCLA Bruins of the '70s. And finally,* The Story of Basketball *is the story of the game itself—rules and strategies, exciting game action, and unforgettable moments.*

illustrated with photographs

Random House · New York

THE
STORY
OF
BASKETBALL

BY JOHN DEVANEY

PHOTOGRAPH CREDITS: The All-American Red Heads, 34; Basketball Hall of Fame/Burt Goldblatt, 12, 13, 14, 16 top, 17, 19 bottom, 21, 24, 31, 32 top; The Frank J. Basloe Family, 3 right, 18; The Bettmann Archive, Inc., 15; The City College of New York, 55 bottom; Culver Pictures, Inc., 16 bottom; D'Ambra Collection, University of Kansas, 26 both, 78 bottom; Delta State College, 137; Malcolm W. Emmons, reverse of front endpaper, 2 both, 3 left, 9, 10 left, 83, 90, 92, 101, 105, 106, 121, 122, 132, 134 left, 140, 143, 146 both, 147 both; Focus On Sports/Lawrence Berman, 118, 131, 133; Focus On Sports/Michael J. Palermi, 100; Focus On Sports/Jerry Wachter, endpapers; The Harlem Globetrotters, 51; Bill Jennaro, 10 right; Purdue Sports Information, 28; Fred Roe, 89 bottom; Stanford University, 36; Syracuse University, 25; Underwood & Underwood, 23 bottom, 27; United Press International, 1 both, 5, 11 right, 22, 37, 38, 39, 40, 43, 45, 48 bottom, 52, 53, 57, 58 center, 59, 62, 63, 64, 65, 66, 69 both, 71, 72, 75 both, 78 top, 79, 89 top, 91, 93, 95, 96, 97, 104, 110, 112, 114, 115, 116, 117, 119, 124 both, 126, 127, 128, 129 both, 134 right, 135, 141, 145; West Virginia University, 81; Wide World Photos, 11 left, 19 top, 23, 30, 32 bottom, 33, 35 both, 41, 42 both, 44, 46, 47, 48 top, 49, 50, 54, 55 top, 58 left & right, 60, 68, 73, 76, 80, 82, 84, 86, 88, 98, 102, 103, 107, 109, 111, 113, 120, 138, 142, 144.

COVER: Photo by Malcolm W. Emmons

Designed by Murray M. Herman

Library of Congress Cataloging in Publication Data
Devaney, John.   The story of basketball.   Includes index.
SUMMARY: Traces the history of basketball including biographical sketches of fourteen players and coaches.
1. Basketball—History—Juvenile literature. 2. Basketball—United States—History—Juvenile literature. 3. Basketball—Biography—Juvenile literature. [1. Basketball—History. 2. Basketball—Biography] I. Title.
GV883.D48   796.32'3'0973   76-8129
ISBN 0–394–82806–2   ISBN 0–394–92806–7 lib. bdg.

Manufactured in the United States of America   1 2 3 4 5 6 7 8 9 0

For my three high scorers— **Barbara, John, and Luke**

Contents

Acknowledgments

Over the years millions of words have been written about the game of basketball, and I have looked at many of those words in assembling this story of the game. Invaluable to anyone tracing the history of the National Basketball Association is Leonard Koppett's *24 Seconds to Shoot*. *The Modern Encyclopedia of Basketball*, edited by Zander Hollander, contains precise summaries of the later years of college and pro basketball. I found these books filled with excellent descriptions of players, games, and other events: *Basketball's Greatest Stars*, by Al Hirshberg; *Stars of Pro Basketball*, by Lou Sabin and Dave Sendler; and *Great Moments in Pro Basketball*, by Dave Wolf and Bill Bruns. I am indebted to the reporting and writing of Peter Carry in *Sports Illustrated* as well as to numerous writers in *Sport* magazine and *The Sporting News*. For his generous assistance I should thank Nick Curran, director of public relations for the National Basketball Association, and for her imaginative editorial guidance, Teddy Slater of Random House.

THE
STORY
OF
BASKETBALL

1

America's Game

You are looking at some of the millions of Americans who play basketball. You are also looking at some of the millions of Americans who watch the game each year. Basketball attracts more American players and fans than any other sport.

Basketball is truly America's Game. The thump of a basketball first echoed in an American gym. Today the basketball hoop is part of the American landscape. It hangs over black-topped driveways in every suburb and stares down on concrete playgrounds in every city. From autumn to spring, the shrill blast of the referee's whis-

A game for everyone: the pros . . .   *. . . the amateurs . . .*

tle is heard across the nation—in high school gyms, college field houses, and big-city arenas.

America gave its game to the world. A year after the first game was played here, boys and girls in Japan were lofting balls at baskets. And before long, basketball was being enjoyed in almost every part of the globe.

The early days of most sports are lost in history, but we can pinpoint the exact time and place that basketball was first played. *The Story of Basketball* began in Springfield, Massachusetts, almost 100 years ago.

. . . the collegians . . .   *. . . and the fans.*

2

"Let's Call It Naismith Ball"

On a winter day in 1891, Jim Naismith snapped his fingers and cried, "I've got it!" After much hard thought, Jim believed that he'd finally found the answer to a question that had been puzzling him for weeks. The question was this: Could Jim think up a game that could be played in a small gym by 18 high-spirited young men without blood being spilled?

Jim Naismith was teaching a course in physical exercise at the Young Men's Christian Association Training School in Springfield, Massachusetts. By steamboat, train, or horse and buggy, derby-hatted young men arrived at this school from all over the world. Here they learned how to be physical-training instructors or business administrators for YMCAs back in their hometowns.

As a child, Jim had always enjoyed sports, especially football. When he grew up, he studied religion in college and earned the degree of doctor of divinity. He considered becoming a minister but finally decided to teach athletics. "I can influence more young men to be good Christians through sports than by preaching to them," he told a friend.

But now, after several months at the Springfield training school, Jim was having trouble interesting his students in athletics. "This new generation of young men wants the pleasure and thrills of games rather than the body-building benefits of exercise," his supervisor had told Jim. "They rebel at tumbling, push-ups, working out with Indian clubs, and other calisthenics. I want you to come up with a game that will give them the exercise they need in the gym during the winter months when we can't go outdoors for football or baseball."

In the weeks that followed, Jim taught his class how to play such games as prison-

Jim Naismith, "The Father of Basketball," invented the game in 1891.

er's base, sailors' tag, and leapfrog, as well as some new games he'd dreamed up himself. To men in their twenties, those games were kid stuff. They laughed scornfully and threw up their hands when Jim demonstrated the games. But when Jim let the students fly at each other in body-bumping games such as soccer, the players limped off the floor clasping bloody heads.

Now, sitting in his room at the school, Jim thought he'd finally come up with the perfect solution—a game that would be exciting but safe. It would be a ball game, but the players would *not* be allowed to run with the ball. "If a player can't run with the ball," he reasoned, "we don't have to tackle. And if we don't have to tackle, the roughness will be eliminated."

But then he wondered: How would a player score a goal? The first thing he thought of was a goal like the one used in lacrosse. In lacrosse a player tries to hurl a ball into a boxlike space. However, Jim realized that if he placed a box on the floor, the defenders could mass in front of it to block the ball. The game would surely get rough. Jim turned over some other ideas in his mind and came up with a good one. He'd hang the box above the heads of the defenders. Then the players couldn't wall off the goal with their bodies.

Now Jim had to decide on the appropriate ball to use. A football, he knew, was shaped to be carried. In his game, however, the players would not be allowed to carry the ball. So Jim chose to use a round soccer ball, which would be more difficult to tuck under the arm.

The next morning Jim walked toward the gym holding a soccer ball. On his way, he happened to meet Mr. Stebbins, the school's janitor. Jim needed two boxes to use as goals. Did Mr. Stebbins happen to have any?

"No," the janitor said. "I haven't any boxes. But I'll tell you what I do have. I have two old peach baskets down in the storeroom—if they will do you any good."

Jim thought the baskets would do just fine. He hung them at opposite ends of a balcony that circled the gym. The bottom of the balcony hung ten feet above the floor. And ever since Jim nailed those peach baskets to that ten-foot-high balcony, basketball hoops have been ten feet high—no more, no less.

At 11:30 that morning, Jim's students filed into the gym for their class. "Huh!" grumbled one student, seeing the baskets. "Another new game!"

"Just try this one game," Jim said. "If you don't like it, I promise I won't try to invent another one."

Jim had the 18 students choose up teams, 9 on a side. Then he asked the captain of each team to stand next to him. He tossed the ball up into the air between the two captains—basketball's first jump ball—and each player tried to snatch the ball. The first game of basketball had begun.

Forbidden to run with the ball, the players passed the ball to teammates or hurled it

The first game of basketball took place in this gymnasium at the YMCA Training School in Springfield, Massachusetts.

Members of the first basketball team pose with Jim Naismith (in suit jacket).

at the peach baskets. Basketball's first players charged across the floor, their shouts and laughter echoing against the wooden walls. They wore long pants and short-sleeved shirts. Sweat ran down their sideburned, mustached faces.

After 30 minutes the students came huffing and puffing off the floor. They were amazed by the new game's excitement and difficulty. Tossing the ball into those peach baskets was much harder than it had looked. By one account only one goal was scored. With 18 bodies zigzagging across the small gym, passing the ball had been a feat of timing and marksmanship. The students flocked around Jim Naismith and asked when they could play this new game again.

During the next week they played often. Their laughter and pounding feet drew visitors to the balcony. In January 1892, after the YMCA students returned from Christmas vacation, other teams were organized at the training school. One team played a

team from a nearby YMCA, the first game between two schools. Most of these early games were won by scores like three goals to two and two goals to one.

In March of that year the students at the YMCA school organized the first basketball tournament. Watching the tournament games from the balcony was a group of women secretaries and students. Someone suggested that they form two teams and play a game. After the men finished their game, the women came onto the floor. In their long flowing dresses, the women tossed the ball at the peach baskets with the same enthusiasm the men had shown.

All winter long, men and women played basketball in the gym. When spring came, they moved outdoors as usual. And they took the new game with them. Outdoors the baskets were hung on poles, and the players ran after the ball on a dirt field.

One spring day a student named Frank Mahan came into Jim's office.

"Dr. Naismith," he said, "what name do you plan to give to the new game?"

Jim said he hadn't given much thought to naming the game.

"How about Naismith ball?" Mahan suggested.

Jim laughed. "That name," he said, "would kill any game."

Mahan tried again. "Why not call it basketball?" he asked. After all, the game was played with a ball and two baskets.

"That would be a good name for it," Jim agreed.

America's Game had a name.

Perched on a stepladder, a man gets set to fish the ball out of the peach basket.

3

The Cagers

In October 1892, only ten months after Jim Naismith tossed up the first jump ball, a friend of his reported on the growing popularity of basketball. He wrote: "It is doubtful whether a gymnastic game has ever spread so rapidly over the continent as has 'basketball.' It is played from New York to San Francisco and from Maine to Texas, by hundreds of teams in associations, athletic clubs, and schools. . . . Naismith is now at work on a new edition of the rules which will shortly be published as 'Basketball for 1893.'"

It was hardly surprising that the new game caught on so quickly. During the 1890s, more Americans lived on farms or in small towns than in cities. In spring and summer, barefoot kids ran on dusty lots or rolling fields to play their games. But when winter winds drove them indoors, their only playground was a town's YMCA gym. The typical dimly lit and musty gym, studded with leather-and-iron exercise bars, looked more like a torture chamber than a place for fun and games. But the excitement of basketball lured the youngsters inside the

gyms. YMCA officials across the country read about Jim Naismith's new game or heard about it from his students when they came home from summer vacations.

Basketball-mania swept the nation. By 1893 many YMCAs had formed basketball leagues. By horse and buggy or trolley car, teams jounced from town to town to play one another. That year, a Nashville, Tennessee, YMCA team beat the Vanderbilt University team, and a Minneapolis Y edged Hamline College, 13 goals to 12. American girls and women joined in the fun, too. Dressed in knee-length bloomer outfits, women at Vassar and Smith colleges tossed balls at baskets during their physical education classes.

Baskets were nailed up in gyms around the globe. The game was carried to foreign lands by training school students sent to overseas YMCAs. By 1894 the game was being played in 15 different countries.

The first men's intercollegiate game took place on February 9, 1895, when the Minnesota State College of Agriculture triumphed over Hamline College, nine goals

15

Women from Smith College show off their new basketball uniforms (1896) . . .

to "pass" the ball at the floor. Then they'd grab the ball on the rebound. And so began what Naismith called one of the game's "prettiest" plays—the dribble.

There were changes in the game's equipment, too. Sporting goods manufacturers turned out special "basketballs." These balls were slightly larger than soccer balls. Stuffed inside their leather cover was a rubber balloon. This balloon—or bladder—was filled with air to give the ball its bounce. The ball was laced, so the bladder could be removed for patching. The new ball was an improvement over the soccer ball, but it was hardly perfect. When the ball hit the floor on its laces, it hopped up at a cockeyed angle. And when the leather ball had been bounced too often, it tended to get lumpy.

By 1897 Jim Naismith's peach baskets had been replaced by net baskets that looked

to three. And later that year a group of women from Smith College played a women's team from Vassar.

During the spring of 1896, the YMCA held a "Championship of America" tournament in Brooklyn. New York's East District Y became the first champs.

A year later, on March 20, 1897, the first college game with five men on a side was played. Yale beat the University of Pennsylvania, 32–10. Each basket now counted as two points and each free throw as one.

That change in the scoring was one of a number of changes that Naismith had made in his original rules. By 1900 the free-throw line was marked 15 feet from the hoop, where it still is today. The keyhole and foul lane were painted on court floors. And teams played two 20-minute halves, as college teams still do.

One of Naismith's original rules had required the players to pass the ball and not run with it. Some clever Yale players began

. . . and men from Columbia University practice their shooting (1910).

The evolution of the basketball hoop—from 1891 (top left) to the present (bottom).

like butterfly nets. When the ball plunked into the net for a goal, the game was stopped. The ball was fished out of the net—sometimes by a man perched on a stepladder. One basket had a cord dangling from it. When the cord was yanked, the ball popped out of the basket. Finally, in 1905, someone made a hoop with an open-bottom net so the ball would drop straight through to the floor after going through the hoop.

The first backboards were put up by Jim Naismith. He placed wire screens behind his peach baskets so that spectators kneeling on the balcony couldn't help their favorite team by steering its shots into the baskets. By the early 1900s, wooden backboards were mounted above the baskets to help players bank the ball into the hoop. In 1910, as crowds began to squeeze into gyms to see the games, some backboards were made of glass so fans seated behind the hoops could watch the action. And there were plenty of fans!

By the turn of the century, the first cries of "We're number one" echoed across college campuses. In 1901 a group of eastern colleges banded together into a league. Yale won the first title. By 1906 Big Ten teams were battling for their own basketball championship. The University of Chicago won

the race three years in a row—from 1908 to 1910. Chicago's John Schommer curled in an average of ten points a game to lead the Big Ten in scoring. From 1911 to 1914 Indiana's Wabash College claimed the number one spot, winning 66 of 69 games.

For some players the honor of being number one wasn't basketball's only reward. In 1898 a pro basketball league, called the National Basketball League, was formed. The pros played for money as well as for glory. One pro team, the Buffalo Germans, won 111 straight games from 1907 to 1911. The Germans' streak was snapped by another team from upstate New York, the Troy Trojans, whose stars were Lew and Ed Wachter. During the winter of 1914–15 the Trojans (also known as the Wachter Wonders) traveled as far west as Montana, winning every game on their 38-game tour. But it wasn't just the number of games the Wachter Wonders won that made them so special—it was the way they won them. Introducing two new plays to basketball—the

FRANK BASLOE ▪close-up▪

One evening during the winter of 1911, 16-year-old Frank Basloe stood on a street corner in Herkimer, New York, watching the grownups stream into the town's dance hall. Frank wished he had 25 cents to buy a ticket. He liked to watch the Saturday night basketball games that were played in these halls before the dancing began. As much as Frank enjoyed watching the games, there was something he enjoyed even more—playing.

A fine player himself, Frank decided to organize his own team. The next day he wrote to Lew Wachter, who played for the Trojans in nearby Troy. He offered Lew five dollars a game if Lew would take leave of the Trojans to play for Frank's team. Lew agreed.

There was only one problem. Frank didn't have the five dollars to pay Lew. But he wasn't about to let that stop him. One freezing, windy day he walked from door to door through Herkimer seeking donations for his team. By nightfall he had a red nose and four dollars. He borrowed another ten dollars from his mother. With the fourteen dollars he bought himself a uniform, sent five dollars to Wachter, and hired three other players. Then he bought train tickets to nearby Ogdensburg. When he and his players clambered onto the train, only a few coins jingled in Frank's pocket.

That night, at a dance hall in Ogdensburg, Frank and his teammates beat the local team, 16–10. After the game Frank hurried to the box office. The dance hall owner gave Frank some of the money taken in for tickets, and Frank used it for train fare to another town.

For six days Frank's team leapfrogged across the state, playing teams in one dance hall after another. At the end of the week the weary players rode back to Herkimer. As the train pulled into the station, Frank saw his father standing on the platform. His father looked angry.

The minute Frank stepped down from the train, his father began shouting at him. "What right have you to take ten dollars of your mother's savings?" Mr. Basloe demanded. "I'll teach you," he said, waving his cane.

"Wait, Poppa," cried Frank, pulling a wad of bills from his pocket. "We made three hundred dollars," he said, pushing the bills toward his father.

Mr. Basloe's frown turned into a smile. His son had earned more money in a week than he could earn in six months. This newfangled basketball was popular—and profitable!

The Buffalo Germans, one of the first pro teams, won 111 games in a row.

bounce pass and the fast-break—they quickened the tempo of the game and made it more exciting than ever.

Watching basketball teams like the Wachter Wonders became a new entertainment for young Americans. In the United States of those years, there were no TV sets or radios. Silent movies could be watched only in the nickelodeons of large cities. In small cities and towns people paid to get into vaudeville theaters to watch acrobats, dancers, and comedians perform on a stage. On Saturday nights, young couples strolled to halls to dance. Some dance hall owners decided to offer an added attraction—a basketball game before the dancing began. Basketball became more popular than ever.

Many of those dance halls were located in basements. The air was hot and smoky. Players had to weave around poles and shoot dartlike liners at the hoops to avoid hitting the low ceilings. Spectators ringed the court. When a ball went out of bounds, players from both teams would go dashing after it—sometimes flattening a fan or two in the process. (In those days, an out-of-bounds ball was given to the last player to get a hand on it.)

To protect the paying customers, dance hall owners built wire cages around the court and put the players inside the cages. Now neither the ball nor the players could fly out of bounds. Ball and players bounced off the sides of the cages. With the ball always in play, the game was faster than ever.

In the years that followed, pro basketball became big business, and the players began to leave the dance halls for large armories and fancy arenas. They left the cages behind them. But to this day, basketball players are still known as "cagers."

Protective netting surrounded the court at the Paterson Armory in New Jersey, where American Basketball League games were played in the early 1900s.

4

The Original Celtics

Over 11,000 screaming fans packed a New York City armory one April night in 1921. They were there to witness the opening game of the long-awaited "world series" of professional basketball. Half the crowd cheered and the other half booed as supershooter Nat Holman led his New York Whirlwinds to a decisive 40–27 victory over New York's Original Celtics.

A few nights later the two teams met in another armory for game two of the three-game series. The game was tense from beginning to end. Arguments and fistfights raged in the stands while the two teams battled it out on the court below. Excitement mounted as the lead seesawed back and forth. With only seconds to go, the Celtics had a two-point advantage—but Whirlwind Nat Holman had the ball.

His eyes darting left and right, Holman dribbled toward the corner, looking for an open man. Finally, he saw a Whirlwind veer toward the foul line and whipped the ball crosscourt. But just as Nat's teammate caught the ball, the buzzer sounded. The game ended with the Celtics on top, 26–24. With that win, the Celtics had evened up the series at one victory apiece.

Still arguing, the crowd spilled out onto the street, Whirlwind and Celtic fans each proclaiming their team number one. Thousands of dollars were plunked down as they bet on one team or the other to win the crucial third game. But no third game was ever played. With excitement among the fans running so high, New York City officials feared a riot and canceled the big game.

Ever since the two teams had been formed, New Yorkers had argued their relative merits. Unlike the Whirlwinds, the Original Celtics had not started out as a pro team. In 1914 a Manhattan social club had organized a basketball team and called it the Celtics. That team disbanded in 1917 as many young Americans put on khaki uniforms to fight in France during World War I. When the war ended a year and a half later, returning soldiers yearned for some fun to forget the war's horrors. A Manhattan businessman named Jim Furey figured that most Americans would feel the same way in these postwar years. The economy was booming, and it seemed safe to assume that people would spend some of their money on entertainment, including sports events. So in 1919 Furey organized a pro basketball team. He wanted to call his team the Celtics, but the social club refused to give up their rights to that name. So Furey decided to call his new team the Original Celtics. Of course, Furey's team was not the original team, although he did hire two former Celtics—Pete Barry and Johnny Whitty. Furey had them sign exclusive contracts, which meant they could play only for his team.

Until then, the best players—Nat Holman, Johnny Beckman, the Wachter brothers—had jumped from team to team. In any given week they might play a game in Brooklyn with one team, take a train to Allentown and play with another team, then move on to Scranton and play with still another team. "We hopped from team to team with a train schedule stuffed in our hip pocket," Nat Holman later recalled.

But now Barry and Whitty had signed contracts to play for only one team, the Original Celtics, just as Babe Ruth had signed a contract to play only for the Yankees. With the signing of Barry and

The Original Celtics' all-star line-up included Nat Holman, Pete Barry, and Dutch Dehnert (fourth, fifth, and sixth from left).

Whitty, pro basketball began its long climb out of the basement dance halls and into the big-city arenas.

Furey waved dollar bills in the faces of other players and convinced them to sign exclusive contracts with the Celtics. Before long, he'd assembled a fine team—the best in the world, Celtic fans claimed. But other fans argued that there was a better team right in New York—the Whirlwinds. The Whirlwinds had been formed by another businessman, Tex Rickard. Their big star was Nat Holman, who once dropped in 150 points in three games. A fierce rivalry developed between the two teams throughout the 1920–21 season. The three-game "world series" in April was supposed to settle the question of which team was truly number one, but that had ended in a stalemate after only two games.

By the next season, however, the debate had been resolved. That year Jim Furey convinced Whirlwinds star Nat Holman to join the Celtics. Before long, just about all of the game's best players were wearing the uniform of the Celtics—bull-shouldered Dutch Dehnert, gangling Joe Lapchick, hulking Horse Haggerty, and speedy Davey Banks, Nat Hickey, and Elmer Ripley. Now almost everyone had to agree: The Celtics were better than the Whirlwinds—or any other basketball team.

With Nat Holman on the team for the 1921–22 season, the Original Celtics joined the Eastern League, made up of teams from New York, New Jersey, and Pennsylvania, and walked off with the championship. The following year they started off right where they'd ended, winning their first 13 games. Then they left the league to tour the country. Bouncing from city to city, the Celtics played the best teams in the nation. That year they won 194 of 204 games.

With their all-star line-up, the Original Celtics had to be good. But the Celtics were more than good; they were great. And

NAT HOLMAN ▪close-up▪

Standing on the sidelines of the Henry Street Settlement gym 12-year-old Nat Holman watched the Roosevelt Big Five players float set shots toward the hoop. Outside, on this winter day of 1908, snow fluttered down on the narrow streets of Manhattan's Lower East Side. The streets were lined with dingy tenements. And crammed into those tenements were immigrant families recently arrived from Europe.

Like other kids from the Lower East Side, Nat played stickball and soccer on the bustling streets every spring and summer. In the winters he played basketball at the settlement house gym—when he could. He and the other smaller boys often were pushed off the basketball court by bigger boys, like these players for the Roosevelt Big Five team. He'd play for that team one day, Nat vowed.

During the next year Nat practiced his shooting, passing, and dribbling. One day a playground instructor noticed Nat and invited him to play for the Big Five. By the end of the 1909–10 season Nat was one of the team's highest scorers. He lofted long two-handed set shots that arched like rainbows through the air and into the basket. From the foul line he dipped his knees for the underhanded free throw, gripping the ball with both hands and shoveling it upward toward the hoop. Seldom did he miss.

Nat's ballhandling was as sharp as his shooting. "He could pass a ball through a keyhole," a teammate once said of him. Dribbling the ball like a yo-yo, Nat would often "freeze" the ball late in a game to protect a slim lead. While his opponents tried to snare the ball, Nat would dribble away—sometimes for as long as two minutes.

He urged teammates to run without the ball and try to get open for a pass near the hoop. "It's not what you can do with a ball that counts," he often said. "It's knowing what to do without a ball that's important."

Nat turned pro in 1916, playing for various teams in the East. He later signed with the New York Whirlwinds, then jumped to the rival Original Celtics in 1921.

The high scorer on the star-studded Celtic team, Nat became basketball's highest-paid player. He earned as much as $500 a week at a time when most people's weekly salary was only $20 or $30. But as far as the Celtics—and Nat, himself—were concerned, he was worth every penny of it.

Playing pro basketball in the 1920s was no easy job, and Nat often earned his money the hard way. "To stay in one piece," he once recalled, "you had to wear hip pads, elbow pads, aluminum cups, and knee guards. Even then you weren't safe. The audience would often drop lighted cigarettes from overhanging balconies or trip you as you came running down the court."

Hostile audiences couldn't stop Nat Holman, though, and neither could the game's best players. In his seven years with the Original Celtics, Nat led them to one victory after another. Altogether, Nat and the Celtics won over 90 percent of their games.

While playing with the Celtics, Nat also began coaching the basketball team at the City College of New York. He held that job for almost 40 years. Cutting and swerving as they traced endless loops around the basket, his teams won 70 percent of their games during those years.

"Look to get open when you don't have the ball," Holman told his players, "and when you do have the ball, look for the open man." That was Original Celtic basketball in the 1920s and eastern basketball from Nat Holman's youth to the present day.

the key to their greatness was teamwork. The Celtics fit together as precisely as the wheels inside a clock. On defense, a Celtic would switch off his man to guard an opponent who flashed into the clear. Then a teammate would pick up the man who'd been left open, a maneuver unheard of before the Celtics introduced it. The Celtics worked together on offense, too, polishing the give-and-go play. One Celtic would pass the ball to another, then dart to the basket and catch a return pass for an easy lay-up.

The Celtics brought other new plays to basketball. During one game an opposing guard stationed himself near the foul line to bat away Celtic passes. For a while, the Celtic offense broke down—but not for long. During a time-out, big Dutch Dehnert came up with a plan.

"I'll stand in front of that guard with my back to the basket," he told his teammates. "One of you pass the ball to me. I'll catch it with him behind me—so he can't intercept it or knock it away. Then I'll pass it back to one of you so you can take a shot."

Play resumed. As planned, a Celtic flicked the ball to Dehnert near the foul line. But as Dutch caught the ball, the rival guard leaned over his right shoulder. Dehnert took a long step with his left foot, then pivoted around the guard and dropped in a short hook shot. The pivot play was born.

The Celtics were usually in control of a game from the opening seconds. When a game began, 6-foot-6 Joe Lapchick (considered a giant at that time) nearly always outleaped the other team's center to tap the ball to a Celtic. Immediately the Celtics would begin to cut and swerve, each player trying to shed his man and get open. As soon as Holman or Beckman saw an open man, they'd drill a pass to him for an easy lay-up. And if no one was free, Beckman or Holman would pop in two-handers from outside.

In those days the ball was brought back to midcourt for a center jump after every basket. Again and again Lapchick would

Two of the greatest stars of the 1920s were both Original Celtics: Nat Holman (above) and Joe Lapchick (below).

23

win the tap—and the Celtics would race downcourt for another basket.

"If you hardly ever get the ball," moaned one opposing coach, "how are you going to beat the Celtics? And it seems like they always have the ball."

As Jim Furey and other businessmen had guessed, Americans thronged to see sports events during the 1920s. This was the Golden Age of Sport. Millions idolized baseball's Babe Ruth, football's Red Grange, and boxing's Jack Dempsey. And in basketball, the idols were Nat Holman and the Original Celtics. Huge crowds came to watch them—23,000 for a game in a Cleveland arena, 10,000 and more at New York's Madison Square Garden.

In 1926, after they had toured the nation for three years, the Original Celtics joined the American Basketball League. The ABL had been organized in 1925. It was the first pro basketball league that could be called national. It stretched from New York to Chicago, and its teams played at large arenas in Philadelphia, Detroit, Washington, and Fort Wayne, Indiana.

The Original Celtics ran away from the other ABL teams, winning the league title two years in a row. Bored fans began to stay away from games because the Celtics

always won. To make the league more competitive, the desperate ABL broke up the Celtics and dealt the players to the other teams.

The Original Celtics no longer existed as a team, but they would be remembered as the best of their era. For years, their incredible record of 1,320 wins against only 66 losses would serve as a standard for professional basketball. Nat Holman, Joe Lapchick, and Pete Barry all went to the Cleveland Rosenblums, where they carried on the Celtic tradition. They led the Rosenblums to two straight ABL championships in 1929 and 1930.

By 1930 the stock market had tumbled, and the harsh gray days of the depression spread across the United States. Men stood on street corners and begged for work. With money so scarce, people no longer pushed into arenas to watch sports events. And in 1931 the American·Basketball League shut its doors.

Once more, pro basketball players became the tramps of sports. They hopped from team to team. They played in smoky small-town gyms and arenas. After a few years of glory, pro basketball seemed on its way back downstairs to the basement dance halls.

A record-breaking crowd of 23,000 fans turned out to watch this game between the Rosenblums and the Original Celtics at Cleveland Auditorium.

5

Figure Eights and Fast-Breaks

In the 1920s and 1930s college football All-Americas such as Illinois's Red Grange were famous coast to coast. Boys from New York to California dreamed of growing up to be a Red Grange.

There were plenty of fine All-America basketball players of that era, but not one of them was as well known as Grange. An All-America basketball player of the 1920s like Syracuse's Vic Hanson might well be a hero in the East. But the name Vic Hanson meant nothing to a midwestern fan, who saved his cheers for local stars like Paul Endacott of the University of Kansas.

It wasn't surprising that there were no nationally known superstars in college basketball. Unlike college football teams, which played in huge 100,000-seat stadiums, college basketball teams played most of their games in small gyms on the campus. Often the gym was in the basement of a building. Only a few hundred people could squeeze in to see the games.

With ticket sales so limited, profits were small. A visiting team would get some of the money taken in at the box office, but that wouldn't take the team far.

Colleges simply couldn't afford to send their teams a thousand miles away to play a game, so there were few intersectional games —East team against West team, North team against South team. And college basketball had no national tournament like football's Rose Bowl, where the best teams from all over the country could meet to battle for the championship crown.

Basketball fans argued about which part of the country had the strongest teams. Some said eastern-style basketball was best and others said western-style basketball was

best. But until East and West could actually meet in a playoff, the question of who was number one would remain unanswered.

Eastern-style basketball featured the patient, methodical style of the Original Celtics. Players weaved through patterns like the Figure 8 as they tried to spring into the open for a pass under the hoop. Or a player would pass the ball, then bolt for the basket on the give-and-go play.

With its slow and deliberate Figure 8 offense, the University of Pittsburgh won 21 games without a defeat in 1928. And the St. John's Wonder Five used the give-and-go

Syracuse superstar Vic Hanson was a hero in the East.

attack to win 86 of 94 games from 1927 to 1930.

Western basketball, also known as "racehorse" ball, featured a speedy run-and-shoot offense. As one player explained: "You grab the ball and run lickety-split for the hoop. When you get close to the basket, you let fly the ball."

Playing racehorse basketball in 1929, Montana State won 35 games and lost only 2. To slow down the racehorse teams, some coaches, such as the University of Kansas's Phog Allen, stationed their players in a zone defense. Instead of guarding a specific player, a Kansas defenseman would guard a specific area, or zone, of the court. The zone defense clogged the area around the basket and made the run-and-shoot play difficult to execute. Rival teams had to stop and shoot over the zone.

To break up the zone, some teams tried to draw the defenders away from the basket. Such teams would stand near the midcourt line and blithely toss the ball back and forth for minutes at a time, a perfectly legal

Kansas coach Phog Allen drills his players on the fine art of defense.

maneuver in those days. "Stall ball," as it was called, often did the trick. The frustrated defensive players would leave their zone and try to steal the ball. But stall ball also frustrated the fans, who'd come to see a game of basketball—not a game of catch.

Basketball in the 1920s and '30s was not a very high-scoring game under the best

PHOG ALLEN ■close-up■

During the 1920s and 1930s, the most famous basketball coach in America was Forrest C. "Phog" Allen of the University of Kansas. In 1922 and 1923 his Jayhawks won 33 of 36 games and were proclaimed the national champions.

Phog (he got the name because of a foghorn voice that blasted constantly at referees) had been a player for Kansas way back in 1906. His coach then had been Jim Naismith, who had come to Kansas to be a professor. Jim hadn't really wanted to be the team coach. "You don't teach basketball," he said, "you play it."

Jim was appalled to see large crowds watch the Original Celtics in the 1920s. "There shouldn't be ten thousand people watching ten people play basketball," he said. "It should be the other way around. Ten people should watch ten thousand play basketball."

In 1908 Phog Allen replaced Jim as the Kansas coach and had a long, successful career. By the time he retired in 1956 he had scored 771 victories in 1,004 games and had won an armful of championship trophies. But one of his proudest possessions was a picture of Jim Naismith with this inscription: "From the father of basketball to the father of basketball coaching."

of circumstances. Stall ball games often ended with scores of 6–4 or 3–1. But even the best racehorse teams rarely racked up more than 50 points a game. In 1929, the top scorers in the country averaged only 12 points a game and final scores of 20–18 and 25–20 were the norm.

One reason for the low scoring was the center jump after each basket. Although the clock kept running, neither team could score while the ball was marched to the midcourt and tossed up into the air. The laced—and lumpy—leather ball of the time didn't help either. When a player tried to bank in a shot, the ball would often bounce at an odd angle and fly by the rim.

To speed up the game—and boost the scoring—a new rule was passed for the 1932 college basketball season. Now the ball had to be brought across the midcourt line within ten seconds—a rule that still stands.

Some young coaches wanted a faster game. "Get rid of the center jump after each basket," they said. "Let a team toss out the ball from under its hoop after it has given up a basket."

Older coaches disagreed. "This game of basketball is almost forty years old," they said. "And what was good enough for Dr. Jim Naismith in 1891 is good enough for us."

One coach who was determined to speed up the game was Ward Lambert, whom everyone called Piggy because he was small and round. Lambert taught his Purdue Boilermakers a modern version of the fast-break that Ed Wachter's Troy Trojans had used to speed to the hoop.

Piggy's best player was a swift guard who ran, Piggy claimed, "like he had an outboard motor attached to him." This player was not as famous as football's Red Grange, because he played most of his games in his own backyard—the state of Indiana. But in that state, which had become wild about basketball, almost every boy yearned to play like the India Rubber Man—Johnny Wooden.

Members of the 1932 Columbia University team warm up before a game.

27

6

Johnny Wooden: The India Rubber Man

"Here comes the India Rubber Man!" someone in the crowd yelled.

Johnny Wooden of Purdue University raced for the hoop, dribbling the ball in front of him. At the foul line he sailed high into the air and flipped a hook shot toward the basket. The ball dropped through the net. Johnny flew toward the seats behind the basket. Three husky spectators—Purdue football players—jumped up, grabbed him in midflight, and tossed him back toward the court. Johnny landed on both feet and bounded toward the other end of the court. The crowd laughed and cheered for Johnny Wooden, the Purdue guard known all over Indiana as the bouncy India Rubber Man.

Johnny had been the idol of boys all over Indiana ever since his high school days. He'd grown up in Martinsville, a small town with one main street, one movie theater, and many dusty lots. Martinsville had little to offer in the way of entertainment. The town's population was 5,200, but when Martinsville High played a basketball game, 5,520 fans packed the school gym to cheer the team to victory.

"Basketball was the *only* sport," Johnny once said. When it came to baseball or football, little towns like Martinsville didn't have enough players in a high school of a hundred or so boys to beat the bigger schools. But a school needed only five players to form a basketball team. And one good player could carry a small-town team all the way to the finals for the state championship.

At tournament time in small towns across Indiana, the streets were empty. Stores closed their doors. People sat hunched close to their new radios and listened for news of the games. Thousands of fans drove

Purdue's Johnny Wooden was known throughout the Midwest as "The India Rubber Man."

Model T Fords down dirt roads to Indianapolis to see their teams fight for the title.

In the spring of 1927 Johnny and his Martinsville High teammates inched their way up through the tournament to face Muncie Central in the finals. Muncie had many more students than little Martinsville High—but they didn't have a player who could compare with Johnny Wooden. With Johnny zipping past opponents on drives to the basket and arching in long two-handed set shots from outside, Martinsville edged out Muncie, 26–23. When Johnny and his teammates came back to Martinsville the next day, they were greeted by a brass band and the cheers of the entire town.

The following year Martinsville again thrilled the town by reaching the state finals. And again their opponents were the boys from Muncie Central. The championship game was close from beginning to end. With only seconds to go, Martinsville took a 12–11 lead. But in the final center jump, the Muncie center tapped the ball to himself, then heaved it at the basket from midcourt. The ball swept through the hoop as the buzzer sounded, and Martinsville was defeated, 13–12.

"That loss taught me to be philosophical about winning and losing," Wooden later recalled. "The difference can be very thin."

From Martinsville Johnny went to Purdue, where he continued to shine. Although he was only 5-foot-10, he could leap high enough to put both hands over the rim of the basket. And his two-handed set shots seemed to be magnetically drawn to the basket. In 1930 and '31 he was named to the college All-America teams. And in 1932 he and the fast-breaking Purdue Boilermakers won 17 of 18 games to capture the Big Ten championship. That same year, Johnny led the Big Ten in scoring (with a 13-point average) and was named All-America for the third year in a row.

Had Johnny been a football player with those credentials, his future would have been bright as can be. He might have been offered as much as $5,000 to play for an NFL team like the Chicago Bears. But there was no pro basketball league around when Johnny graduated from Purdue.

If he wanted to play basketball now, Johnny would have to join a semi-pro team. Semi-pro players worked at regular jobs during the day and played for money at night or on weekends. Johnny already had a daytime job coaching high school basketball. He also coached the school's baseball and tennis teams and taught English—all for $25 a week. A semi-pro team asked Johnny to play for it, and Johnny agreed. So Purdue's three-time All-America began to play for the Indianapolis Kautsky Grocers.

Late in the 1935–36 season Johnny stood at the foul line in a tiny arena in Kokomo, Indiana. Some 1,500 people watched expectantly as he gripped the ball with two hands. So far that season Johnny had dropped in 99 straight free throws for the Kautsky Grocers. Aiming for his 100th in a row, he arched the seamed leather ball upward. A thunderclap of noise shot across the smoky arena as the ball dropped through the net.

Frank Kautsky, the groceryman who owned the team, came onto the court and handed Johnny a $100 bill, one dollar for each of his 100 free throws. Johnny stood there grinning. It was the first $100 bill he had ever seen!

That scene in Kokomo typified the world of pro basketball in the 1930s and on into the 1940s. Games were played in these small arenas by men wearing worn, faded uniforms. Veteran players looked like boxers, their faces flattened and bruised. Fists and elbows swung under the basket during every game. The paying customers cheered when punches were thrown, so the referees blew the whistle at only the most flagrant fouls. "No blood, no whistle" was an unstated rule. Fights broke out in the stands as well as on the court. And when the home team lost, referees and visiting players sometimes needed a police escort out of town to shield them from the angry fans.

Teams had such names as the Brooklyn Visitation Triangles, the Fort Wayne Zollners, and the Akron Goodyear Tires. Teams were sponsored by social clubs or business firms. The players often had to drive hundreds of miles in their cars to get to a game. They carried their own sneakers, tape, and basketball. On many Monday mornings Johnny Wooden walked bleary-eyed into the South Bend Central High to teach an English class after having driven all night from a game in Oshkosh or Sheboygan.

By 1933, as politicians promised that

"prosperity was just around the corner," Americans began to hope that the most frightening days of the Depression were behind them. That year the old American Basketball League reopened its doors. But it bore little resemblance to the league that had stretched from New York to Chicago during the free-spending days of the 1920s when its big attraction was the Original Celtics. Now the ABL was made up of teams on the East Coast that were within a cheap bus ride of each other. In the 1930s and '40s the Philadelphia Sphas, representing the South Philadelphia Hebrew Association, won the ABL title seven times in thirteen seasons.

In 1937 a rival league was formed in the Midwest. It was called the National Basketball League. Like Johnny Wooden (who retired in 1938 as a player to become a coach at Indiana State) most NBL players worked during the day and played for a team at night. The first NBL champions in the 1937–38 season were the Akron

The Oshkosh All-Stars and the Detroit Eagles battle for the 1942 NBL championship.

The Philadelphia Sphas dominated the American Basketball League during the 1930s and '40s, winning seven championships in thirteen seasons.

Goodyear Tires. Another company-sponsored team, the Akron Firestones, won the title in 1939. From 1940 to 1946 the NBL championships were won by such teams as the Oshkosh All-Stars, the Fort Wayne Zollners, and the Rochester Royals.

Sports fans in big cities heard those team names and thought of pro basketball as a minor-league game. But in the summer of 1946 still another league would be formed —and pro basketball would join baseball and football as a truly major-league sport.

7

On Tour

Playing for a National Basketball League team such as the Oshkosh All-Stars was hardly the big time. But there were many fine basketball players of the 1930s who were denied even that opportunity for a pro career—namely women and blacks. Nevertheless, some of the most exciting ball of that era was played by those very athletes.

While most pro basketball teams of the 1930s stuck to a region—the Kautsky Grocers played in the Midwest, the Philadelphia Sphas on the Eastern Seaboard— some other teams hopped around the

country the way the Original Celtics had toured in the twenties. Two of these teams were made up of black players, and a third was an all-women team.

The two all-black teams were rated among the nation's best—pro or college—and the better of these teams was the New York Renaissance Big Five, also known as the Rens. During one cross-country swing, the Rens won 88 straight games. In 1935 and '36 the Rens played Johnny Wooden and his Kautsky Grocers team in a series of games across Indiana. The Rens won that

The New York Rens were organized by Robert Douglas (inset) in 1922. The most popular Rens were Bill Yancy (second from left) and Wee Willie Smith (far right).

series and made a fan out of Johnny Wooden, who called the Rens "the best team I ever saw."

Center for the Rens was "Wee Willie" Smith, a muscular 6-foot-5 heavyweight. "He was the meanest player I ever saw," Wooden recalled. "Whenever he got into a fight, it was over right now. I'm not ashamed to say I was scared of him."

Popping in two-handed set shots was the Rens' Bill Yancey. "Even with a ball that was none too round in those days, he would hit every shot from nine different positions," said Wooden. "I saw him do it, moving from one corner to the other and back, eighteen times in a row without missing a shot."

In their best years—from 1932 to 1936 —the Rens won 473 games while losing only 49. And they played the best white teams in every city they visited. But good as they were, the Rens never attained the popularity of another black team that toured the country at the same time—the Harlem Globetrotters.

The Globetrotters first began to trot in 1927. Basketball promoter Abe Saperstein —who was shaped a bit like a basketball

himself—organized some black players in Chicago. "We're going to travel," the stocky promoter told his players. "So let's call ourselves the Harlem Globetrotters."

A friend protested. "Not one of your players has ever been to Harlem," he pointed out. "And how can you call yourselves Globetrotters? Most of these players have never been out of Chicago."

Abe Saperstein, owner-coach of the Harlem Globetrotters, later bought the Rens.

"That's the idea," Abe said, a shrewd smile on his face. "Harlem identifies the boys as a Negro team. And Globetrotters makes it sound as if they've been around."

Abe and his players piled into an old jalopy. They chugged out of Chicago and rolled to their first stop in Hinckley, Illinois. Abe located the owner of a local basketball team and arranged for a game that night. The Globetrotters won, collected their share of the box-office money ($75), then rattled off to another town. In their first season (1927–28) the Globetrotters won 101 games and lost only 6.

They played anywhere and everywhere. In Montana they once played a game in an empty swimming pool. There was one basket at the shallow end and one at the deep end. The players had to run downhill toward one hoop and uphill toward the other. In a tiny Wisconsin hall a Globetrotter leaped for a rebound and banged his head against the low ceiling. In Iowa the team played one game in a barn heated by a potbellied stove. A Globetrotter plopped down on the hot stove, then made a beeline for the dressing room with his pants smoking. But no matter where they played, one thing never changed. The Globetrotters overwhelmed most of the teams they challenged.

Saperstein began signing the best black players in the country, and the Globetrotters got better and better. In one game in Canada they ran up a 112–5 lead! The bored Globies asked Abe if they could clown around with the ball to amuse the spectators and themselves. Abe agreed. Moments later Willie Oliver let the ball slide down his skinny arms. Runt Rollins began to tap dance as he dribbled. The crowd laughed and yelled for more stunts.

One of the new Globies was Reece "Goose" Tatum. The 6-foot-3 Tatum had long arms that dangled at his knees when he ran. He got his nickname when one of the Globies said he looked like a goose flapping his wings. The Goose's favorite stunt was to get to a gym early, plop into a seat under the basket, and disguise himself as a spectator by grabbing someone's hat and overcoat. When the Globies got the ball, Goose would hop out of the seat, wave his arms for the ball, grab a long pass, and happily stuff the ball through the hoop.

By 1938 the Globies were the most famous basketball team in the nation. They

Globie Reece Tatum was nicknamed "The Goose" because of his long, dangling arms.

amused fans in small-town gyms and in the huge Madison Square Garden. They made Abe Saperstein a millionaire. Saperstein used some of that money to buy the New York Rens. Then he moved the best Rens to the Globetrotters. But years later all the members of those 1932–36 Rens got the recognition that was never given to them in their prime. The whole team was elected to the Basketball Hall of Fame.

Also vagabonding around the country during the 1930s were the All-American Red Heads. Made up of the best high school and college women players an Arkansas businessman could find, the Red Heads dyed their hair red and wore flashy star-spangled red, white, and blue uniforms. In a typical year the team traveled 60,000 miles—the equivalent of 20 trips from New York to Los Angeles.

The Red Heads played against the best men's teams in the cities and towns they visited. Like the Globetrotters, they clowned during portions of their games—but only when they were leading. And like the Globetrotters, the All-American Red Heads seldom lost. In one season they racked up 188 wins against only 13 defeats.

While the Red Heads, the Rens, and the Globetrotters were touring the country in the late 1930s, a young black basketball player was setting scoring records at the University of California at Los Angeles (UCLA). He would later become more famous as a big-league baseball player. After

The All-American Red Heads challenged men's teams all over the country.

him, black players would stream through the doors of big-league locker rooms in every sport. His name was Jackie Robinson. And although Jackie would not live to see it, there would also come a day when women athletes in every sport would begin to receive rewards and recognition.

8

East Meets West

The balding 29-year-old Ned Irish toyed with his glasses as he watched the crowds of people swarming into the Manhattan College gym one wintry night in 1933. Ned, a sportswriter, had been sent there to write about this game for his newspaper. But he couldn't push his way inside. The gym was packed.

Ned saw an open basement window. As he squirmed through, he heard a loud ripping sound. He'd torn his pants. But he wiggled inside, watched the game, and came back to his newspaper with the story.

Later he reflected on the popularity of college basketball in New York. In 1920 some 10,000 people had crowded into an armory to watch City College of New York play New York University. As recently as 1931, a college basketball triple-header had filled the 18,000 seats of Madison Square Garden. Yet each season, Ned well knew, NYU, Manhattan, CCNY, and other New York college teams played most of their games in tiny campus gyms before overflow crowds.

Ned thought: Why not move those games into the roomy Madison Square Garden? The New York Rangers and other hockey teams played in the Garden during the winter, but there were many nights when the big arena was dark. So Ned arranged for a double-header on December 29, 1934.

That night some 16,000 fans came to the Garden and saw Notre Dame beat NYU, 25–18, and Westminster defeat St. John's, 37–33.

With that success under his belt, Ned quit his job as a reporter and went to work for the Garden, arranging basketball double-headers. He called colleges across the country and invited them to come to the Garden —"the capital of the basketball world," as he called it.

Seven more double-headers were played at the Garden in 1935. The games drew more than 100,000 fans, who willingly paid one and two dollars a ticket to see their favorite teams. The Garden paid some of that money to the college teams. It was more than enough to pay their train fare to and from New York.

By 1936 big arenas in Philadelphia, Chicago, and other cities were inviting college teams to play in double-headers. On the way east, a team from California could stop in a Chicago arena—and at campus gyms spotted along the way—before coming into the Garden. Playing three or four games, they would return home with wallets fat enough to pay for other trips. For the first time, college basketball teams were playing intersectional games—East against West, North against South. And many fans who had not been able to squeeze into small college gyms were seeing college basketball for the first time. Like all fans, they looked for heroes to root for.

Most high scorers of the 1930s were quick, small men who drove for lay-ups or twirled in two-handed set shots from outside. The best of them averaged around 12 points a game. But in 1936 Ned Irish heard about a slim forward at Stanford, on the West Coast, who had tossed in 24 points in one game with a running, *one-handed* shot. The player's name was Angelo "Hank" Luisetti.

Ned invited Stanford to come to the Garden on December 29, 1936, to play

Ex-reporter Ned Irish starts a new career at Madison Square Garden as a basketball promoter.

Long Island University, one of the best teams in the East. When the two teams met, the LIU Blackbirds had 43 straight victories behind them—the nation's longest winning streak.

The Stanford players were not intimidated, though. Early in the game Hank

In 1936 East meets West at the Garden: LIU (New York) vs. Stanford (California).

dribbled toward the keyhole. He was guarded by LIU's All-America, Art Hillhouse. While racing next to Hillhouse, Hank pushed the ball one-handed toward the basket. The ball ripped through the nets.

"I'll never forget that look on Hillhouse's face," Hank said years later. "He'd never seen a shot like that. When it hit I could just see him saying, 'Boy, is this guy lucky!' "

LIU soon found out that Hank had more than luck going for him. Hank didn't take very many shots that night, but the ones he did take were winners. With his one-handers,

Hank swished in 15 points. And Stanford ended LIU's winning streak with a convincing 45–31 triumph.

By the end of that 1936–37 season Stanford had a 25–2 record. And basketball fans had a genuine hero in Hank Luisetti. Wherever Stanford journeyed, fans clamored to see the Luisetti one-hander. In Philadelphia, 11,000 fans packed an arena and thousands more were turned away. In Cleveland a mob of fans tried to rip the jacket off Luisetti's back for a souvenir.

Now that college teams could afford to

HANK LUISETTI ▪close-up▪

The skinny Galileo High School player leaped up and grabbed the rebound. But he came down with his back to the basket. He couldn't take a two-handed shot with his back to the basket. Instinctively, Hank Luisetti took one step backward, then spun and shot the ball with one hand. The ball rippled through the net.

Hank took little notice of that shot—nor did anyone else. He was no high-scoring whiz for this San Francisco high school. Hank averaged only eight points a game, but he was a clever dribbler and passer. In fact, he could do so many things that a Stanford coach offered him a basketball scholarship.

In one game at Stanford in 1935, Hank began to flip one-handers on the run. "It was bang, bang, bang," Stanford coach John Bunn later recalled. Hank scored 35 points. "That one-hander looks weird," the coach told Hank, "but stick with it." Bunn didn't care how weird the shot looked if Hank could score more points in a game than most *teams* of that time could score.

But Hank didn't particularly want to be a high scorer. He had great pride in his defense, dribbling, passing, and rebounding. "I had flash, but I had the whole game," he once said.

In one game against Southern California, Hank tossed in only six points in the first three quarters. USC led by 15 points. "For Pete's sake," coach Bunn yelled, "shoot, Hank, shoot." Hank began to stream one-handers at the hoop. He scored 24 points in the next 11 minutes, and Stanford won, 51–47.

In a game against Duquesne, Stanford was leading by a wide margin. The Stanford players tossed the ball to Hank. When he returned it, they passed it right back to him. "Cut it out," he yelled. But they made him shoot. That night he tossed in a record-breaking 50 points.

In his three years at Stanford, Hank Luisetti scored 1,596 points, more points than any college player before him. That record would soon be smashed, scores clicking higher as the game became faster. But in 1950, when sportswriters voted for the greatest players of the first half-century, Hank Luisetti was ranked second only to the great George Mikan.

"I can't remember anyone who could do more things," LIU coach Clair Bee said at the time. "He was an amazing marksman, a spectacular dribbler, and an awfully clever passer. He was the greatest player I have ever seen."

travel coast to coast, some New York sportswriters thought there should be a national tournament that would decide which team was truly number one. The writers organized the National Invitation Tournament. The first NIT would be held at Madison Square Garden after the 1937–38 season.

In that 1937–38 season, basketball had a new faster look. No longer was there a center jump after each basket. Now the ball was thrown into play immediately after a basket by the team that had been scored upon. With no time wasted taking the ball to mid-court, scoreboards began to click faster. Playing what was called "point-a-minute basketball," teams reeled off 50 and more points in a 40-minute game. Racehorse teams such as Rhode Island State and Purdue often scored 60 and 70 points.

As Hank Luisetti piled up points at a record pace, other players began to imitate his one-handers. They didn't have to weave through complex patterns to get open for a lay-up or a two-handed set shot. And the one-handed shot thrown suddenly was difficult to block.

Old-timers snorted when they saw one-handers. "I'll quit coaching if I have to teach the one-handed shot to win," growled former Celtic Nat Holman, now the CCNY coach. "Nobody can convince me that a shot predicated on a prayer is smart basketball."

Later that season Stanford came back to the Garden—this time to play CCNY—and Hank made a believer out of Holman. In the first half Hank fed the ball to his teammates and scored only six points himself, but Stanford took a commanding lead. In the second half CCNY began to whittle away at the Stanford lead. But then Hank looped 13 successive points through the hoop with his one-handers, and Stanford surged ahead to win, 45–42. "Hank Luisetti blew the game wide open," wrote a reporter the next day.

Stanford finished that season with a 21–3 record but decided not to make the long

Stanford's Hank Luisetti displays his unusual one-handed shooting style.

train ride to the NIT in New York. That first NIT championship was won by Temple, which defeated Colorado, 60–36, in the finals. Because Stanford and other strong teams had stayed away from the NIT, fans still argued about which team was number one. But when it came to picking the greatest college player in the land, there was little disagreement—Hank Luisetti was truly number one.

9
AAU Ball

Warming up on the brightly lit yellow floor of a Denver arena were players for the San Francisco Olympic Club and a team representing the Twentieth Century Fox film company. Within a few minutes these two teams would battle for the 1941 championship of the Amateur Athletic Union, better known as the AAU.

The star of the Olympic team was Hank Luisetti, now out of college. But Hank was still an amateur, not a paid pro. Like most All-Americas of the day, he had joined an AAU team after graduating from Stanford.

Competing in the AAU program were amateur teams representing social and athletic clubs as well as schools and colleges. Many other teams represented commercial businesses. Amateurs are paid no money for playing ball. But even though the players on these company-sponsored teams were paid salaries, they were still considered amateurs. During the day they'd work for the company—often as salesmen or junior executives—and at night they'd play on the company's AAU basketball team. The players were paid for their daytime work, however, not for their ballplaying. When these players got too old to play basketball, they could look ahead to a bright future with the company. For an All-America basketball player, company-sponsored AAU ball had more to offer than the pro teams of the era.

The best AAU teams met in an annual tournament for the championship. The AAU championship is the oldest basketball tournament in the United States. It dates back to 1897, when the first winner was the New York 23rd Street YMCA. In 1913 it became a yearly event.

The AAU also held a national tournament for women's basketball teams. Women had been playing basketball in high school

Des Moines and New Orleans teams fight for the 1947 Women's AAU championship.

and college since Naismith's day. But by the early 1900s some officials had decided that basketball was too strenuous for females. So they developed a modified version of the game just for women. In the new game of women's basketball there were six players on a team—three guards and three forwards. The court was divided into three zones. A team's three guards couldn't cross into a zone covered by its three forwards. And the team's three forwards had to stay out of zones covered by its three guards. As a result, women's basketball was a game of three on three—three forwards against the other team's three guards. The remaining six players had to stand around until the ball bounced into their zones.

Good women athletes hated these hobbling rules. The only way they could play the faster, more exciting game was to join women's AAU teams, which played by men's rules. In 1926 the AAU held its first national championship for women. Winners were former high school and college players who represented the Pasadena (California) Athletic and Country Club.

BABE DIDRIKSON ▪close-up▪

The crowd in the noisy Wichita, Kansas, arena let out a sudden roar. In this 1931 AAU women's championship game, one Dallas Golden Cyclone player had flipped seven successive shots into the basket. Her name was Mildred Didrikson—Babe to everyone who knew her. As she ran upcourt after that seventh straight basket, the grinning Babe raised one fist high in triumph. Minutes later she and her teammates ran off the court the 1931 AAU women's champions.

During the five-game tournament, 19-year-old Babe had poured in a spectacular—but not surprising—total of 106 points for her team. Babe had been doing the spectacular ever since her early childhood in Beaumont, Texas. As a youngster, she'd run barefooted on dusty lots, competing against boys in baseball, football, and whatever other games the gang played. In a time when girls were supposed to stand daintily on the sideline and cheer for the boys, Babe plunged into the action with clenched fists. Years later she advised girls who wanted to be athletes ("and do some winning") to play against boys.

In high school, however, Babe had to play basketball against girls. With the underhanded free throw and the two-handed set shot of the day, she seldom missed. An executive for a Dallas insurance company saw her play. He offered her $75 a month to work for the company and play for its women's team. The team, called the Golden Cyclones, had finished second in the 1929 AAU tournament. With Babe as its captain, it won that 1931 tournament and Babe was named to the women's All-America team.

But basketball wasn't Babe's only game. In 1932 the Cyclones sent only one athlete to represent them at the AAU track championships—Babe Didrikson. They didn't really need anyone else. Babe won five events—the javelin, hurdles, shot put, broad jump, and baseball throw. She also tied for first place in the high jump and came in fourth in the discus throw. She won 30 points for her one-woman team to win the AAU championship. That same year, she went to the Olympics and brought home two gold medals and one silver.

In the years that followed, Babe pitched in an exhibition game against the St. Louis Cardinals. She bowled 200. She dived with a champion's grace and came close to breaking world records in swimming. As a golfer she won 82 major tournaments, including the 1954 National Open when she was ill with cancer. In 1950, six years before she died, she was named the woman athlete of the half-century. A sportswriter once asked her, "Is there anything you don't play?"

"Yeah," replied Ms. Didrikson. "Dolls!"

The men's AAU tournaments became the "World Series" of amateur basketball. When Hank Luisetti and his Olympic Club teammates vied for the 1941 championship, almost 10,000 fans turned out to cheer them on. Although the Olympic Club was defeated by the Twentieth Century Fox team, Hank was unanimously voted the 1941 tournament's most valuable player. "He's the best in the world," said one AAU team's coach. "I want him."

The coach was Chuck Hyatt. His team, the Phillips 66ers (also called the Oilers), was sponsored by the Phillips Oil Company. A typical company-sponsored AAU team, it was organized in 1921 by Kenneth "Boots" Adams, a worker in a Phillips warehouse. By 1940 Boots Adams no longer played for the team, but he was a rising executive. (In 1947 he would be president of the company.) Adams talked All-Americas into coming to work for the company, and he hired so many that the 66ers won the AAU championship in 1940.

After the 1941 tournament Adams spoke to Hank Luisetti. By 1942 Hank was sitting behind a desk in a Phillips office during the day. At night he ran onto a basketball floor in an Oiler uniform. Led by Luisetti, the Oilers came in second in the 1942 AAU tournament, and in the next six years they won six straight championships.

Many experts in the 1940s rated the Oilers superior to any college or pro team in the United States. Naturally, this infuriated the owners of pro teams. The owners sought All-Americas like Hank Luisetti who would draw college basketball fans to the pro games. But the pros kept losing the best college stars to AAU teams such as the Phillips Oilers.

"The Oilers aren't interested in Luisetti as an executive," one pro owner growled. "They're interested in him as a basketball player. We pay our pro players over the table. Those AAU teams give their money to the player under the table."

Playing for the Phillips 66ers in 1941, Hank Luisetti aims for the hoop.

But as long as the pro teams played in smoky back-alley gyms, most All-Americas would choose AAU basketball. To attract the All-Americas, the pros would have to play their games in big arenas, such as Madison Square Garden. That time would come—but it was a world war away.

10

Forecast for the Future

Just before the start of the 1939–40 college basketball season, Jim Naismith died. Almost half a century had passed since he'd tossed up a soccer ball for the world's first game of basketball. In those 50 years, the sport had changed in many ways. But basketball would change even more in the years to come. Events of the 1939, 1940, and 1941 seasons forecast a bright future for America's game.

For the first time ever, a basketball game was televised. In 1940 a New York station telecast a college double-header from Madison Square Garden to the few hundred people who owned TV sets.

In the lobbies of Madison Square Garden and other big-city arenas, gamblers were placing bets of $100 and more on a single game. Before one NIT game at the Garden

an estimated half-million dollars was wagered.

College basketball had a new post-season tournament. It was organized by the National Collegiate Athletic Association, which supervised college athletics. Now the two best college teams—one from the East and one from the West—met in the finals for the NCAA championship. Unlike the NIT, which tended to invite many eastern teams, the NCAA drew teams from each section of the country. Its champion was hailed by most fans as the nation's number one team. When the first NCAA tournament was played in 1939, the western champion, Oregon, defeated the eastern champion, Ohio State, 46–33.

Slick new rubber balls that had no laces replaced the lumpy old leather ones that

In 1939 teams from Ohio State and Oregon compete in the first NCAA tournament.

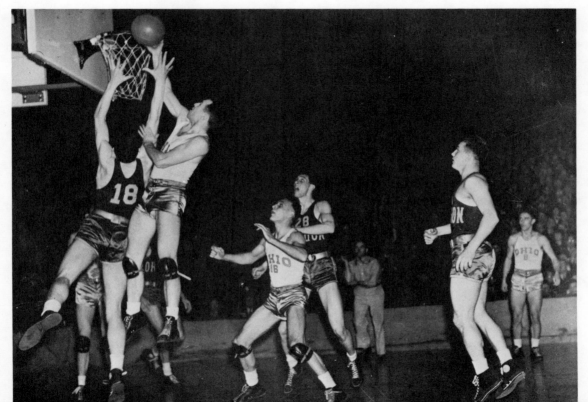

Rhode Island State's Stutz Modzelewski averaged a record-breaking 23 points a game.

Stutz dropped in most of his shots with the two-handed set that was still the most popular outside shot. But at a high school in Tennessee, a 6-foot-5 forward named Joe Fulks was tossing in a one-handed jump shot at a startling rate. Meanwhile, other high school players were copying Hank Luisetti's running one-hander—but only when their coaches weren't looking.

The game's high scorers were still smaller men: Seton Hall's Bob Davies, Ohio University's Frank Baumholtz, UCLA's Jackie Robinson, and North Carolina's George Glomack. In 1941 a Wisconsin forward, Johnny Kotz, put in enough points to lead Wisconsin to 15 straight victories and the NCAA championship.

But rising on the horizon of college basketball was a towering row of giants. In the next few years smaller men would look up at them and wince in dismay as these giants poured in as many as 50 points a game. One of the biggest and best was named George Mikan.

UCLA guard Jackie Robinson was one of the highest-scoring players in the country.

had bounced so unpredictably. Dribblers bounced the new balls behind their backs and between their legs—stunts that had been almost impossible with the old balls. And now shooters could bank the smooth balls off the backboard and into the hoop with more accuracy than ever before.

Scores climbed higher and higher. Frank Keaney's racehorse Rhode Island State team averaged a record-breaking 70 points a game and rang up as many as 100 in one night. Rhode Island's high scorer, Stan "Stutz" Modzelewski, fired in an average of 23 points a game, another record. By the time he graduated, Modzelewski would score 1,730 points and smash Hank Luisetti's college career record.

11

David vs. Goliath

Soldiers in khaki overcoats and sailors in navy blue pea jackets mixed with throngs of civilians as the crowd poured into Madison Square Garden to watch the semi-final round of the 1944 National Invitation Tournament. In the corners of the lobby, thick wads of bills passed from hand to hand as fans bet on their favorite teams.

Outside, on nearby newsstands, black headlines read: "1,000 ALLIED BOMBERS SMASH GERMAN CITIES." Allied armies were poised to invade Europe while American Marines dug into foxholes on Pacific beaches. Around the globe, armies and navies prepared for the climactic battles of World War II.

At home, huge crowds, eager to forget the war for a few hours, packed the Garden to its rafters. This semi-final game was being billed as the "Battle of the Giants," and many fans had come to gawk at two of the biggest men ever to lace on basketball shoes —Bob Kurland of Oklahoma A & M and George Mikan of DePaul University.

Before the game began, a New York reporter spotted Hank Iba, coach of the Oklahoma Aggies. "Well, Hank, what do you think now about having a goon at center?" he asked.

Iba grinned sheepishly. For several years the coach had been complaining that "galloping goons"—as he called the tall centers —would dominate the game and turn it into a sport that only they could play. "How can you stop them?" he'd once protested. "A seven-footer can grab a ball and dunk it into the hoop, and only another seven-footer can stop him."

But now the rueful coach had to admit that it was a "goon" who had brought his team this far. The Aggie center, a hulking redhead named Bob Kurland, stretched seven feet high. People bent their necks to look up at him and nicknamed him "Foothills." Big Bob was a double threat to rival players. On defense he'd stand under the hoop and bat away shots like a hockey goaltender. And Foothills was just as effective on offense. When the Aggies got the ball, they'd patiently wait for their slow-moving center to lumber downcourt, then feed him the ball. Foothills would pivot stiffly, stretch a long arm toward the hoop, and lay the ball in. Below him, his six-foot

The Battle of the Giants: DePaul's George Mikan vs. Oklahoma A & M's Bob Kurland.

Dick Triptow of DePaul drives past his St. John's defenders during the finals of the 1944 National Invitational Tournament.

defenders would stand, helplessly staring at his massive chest.

As Kurland and his teammates prepared to face DePaul, coach Iba told the reporter, "I still think goons will ruin the game if we don't put in rules to control them. But when you've got one, I say use him."

In this semi-final game Hank would need the seven-foot Kurland. DePaul had a giant of its own—6-foot-9 George Mikan. The nearsighted Mikan had to peer at the basket through thick glasses, but when it came time to shoot, he had no trouble seeing the basket. During the regular season he'd averaged 20 points a game.

If the fans at the Garden expected a shoot-out between the two big men, however, they were sadly disappointed in this "Battle of the Giants." Seconds after the referee tossed up the ball for the center jump, it became clear that for tonight, at least, the name of the game was defense. Time after time, the

ponderous 240-pound Kurland and the 235-pound Mikan slammed into each other under the boards.

Both men got into foul trouble early in the game. Minutes into the second half Mikan committed his fifth and was sent to the bench after scoring only nine points. The DePaul Demons kept on running against the tiring Kurland, and with two minutes left on the clock, Kurland also fouled out. He left the game with 14 points. In the final minute of the game DePaul spurted ahead to win, 41–38.

The Demons' victory earned them the right to battle St. John's for the championship. While the semi-final match had been called the "Battle of the Giants," the finals could fittingly be described as "David vs. Goliath."

Coached by former Celtic Joe Lapchick, the fast-breaking St. John's team had been the 1943 NIT champs. Yet most people considered them underdogs in this contest against DePaul. The best players for St. John's were the 5-foot-8 Hy Gotkin and a six-foot freshman, Bill Kotsores. To defeat Mikan and DePaul, Lapchick knew his team would have to rely on strategy instead of strength. So he told his speedy little players to drive straight at Mikan whenever they got the ball. "He'll foul you as he tries to block your shots," Lapchick predicted.

Lapchick's tactic worked perfectly. Harassed by the driving St. John's players, Mikan picked up five fast fouls and left the big game early in the second half. With Mikan out of the way, St. John's unreeled a string of nine straight points to win its second NIT title in a row.

In 1945 Mikan and his DePaul teammates returned to the Garden, still seeking their first NIT title. Their semi-final playoff, against Rhode Island State, was another case of David vs. Goliath. Starring for Rhode Island State was sharp-shooting Ernie Calverley. During the regular season, Calverley had led the nation in scoring with 27 points

a game. But at only 5-foot-11, little Ernie was hardly a match for big George. Mikan ripped a Garden-record 53 points through the hoop, and DePaul triumphed, 97–53. Single-handedly, Mikan had matched the point total of the entire Rhode Island team. In the finals, George contributed 34 points, as DePaul outscored Bowling Green, 71–54, for the NIT crown.

In the opening round of the 1946 NIT the 145-pound Calverley and his Rhode Island teammates once again found themselves looking up to a giant. This time it was 6-foot-11 Don Otten of Bowling Green. Refusing to be intimidated, the plucky Rhode Island players battled Bowling Green right down to the wire. Still, with only two seconds left in the game, Rhode Island trailed 74–72. A Rhode Island player had possession of the ball, but he was almost a full court-length away from Rhodie's hoop.

Desperately, the Rhode Island player looked for an open teammate. He saw the skinny arms of Ernie Calverley flapping wildly at the foul circle and passed the ball

Little Ernie Calverley gets off a jump shot for Rhode Island State during the 1946 NIT final against Bowling Green.

to him. Ernie was three-quarters of the court away from the hoop, but he was the only player open.

As he grabbed the ball, Ernie glanced at the clock and saw there was no time to dribble. He looked at the hoop hanging in the distance. Gripping the ball with both hands, he leaped up and heaved it toward that faraway hoop.

The ball arched through the air of a suddenly hushed Madison Square Garden. Some 18,000 fans held their breath as the ball flew 60 feet before plummeting through the hoop. Then a great roar shook the Garden. Ernie's incredible shot had tied the game.

In overtime Rhode Island swept by the stunned Bowling Green players to win the game. Little Ernie and his teammates had bested the giant Don Otten—and attained revenge for all the points big George Mikan had shoved down their throats a year earlier.

Little Rhodie climbed all the way to the finals, where it played another cliff-hanger, this time against Kentucky. In the last seconds of that game the score was tied, 45-all, when Kentucky's freshman guard, Ralph Beard, dropped in a free throw to win the game—and Kentucky's first NIT championship.

After the 1946 NIT Ned Irish and other big-city basketball promoters couldn't help noticing how more and more Americans,

Coach Frank Keaney and teammate Al Palmieri give Ernie a victory ride after the game.

made affluent by the war, were clamoring to see college basketball games in the big arenas. The names Mikan and Calverley were as well known to sports fans as baseball's Ted Williams and football's Sammy Baugh.

Irish was sure that the fans would want to see these All-Americas play as pros when they graduated. He predicted that fans would crowd into such big-city arenas as Madison Square Garden, Chicago Stadium, and the Philadelphia Palestra to see pro basketball—provided the players were as famous as Mikan and Calverley. It was time, Irish argued, for pro basketball to attempt to become big league.

12

Birth of the NBA

On June 6, 1946, a group of businessmen sat around a long table in a conference room at the Hotel Commodore in New York City. At the head of the table was Ned Irish, now an executive with Madison Square Garden. Around him sat several owners and representatives of other big-city arenas. These

men had come here to form a new pro basketball league. Now they were reviewing the decisions they had made.

The new league would be called the Basketball Association of America (BAA). It would be made up of teams from 11 cities—Boston, Chicago, Detroit, Cleveland,

46

New York, Philadelphia, Pittsburgh, Providence, St. Louis, Toronto, and Washington, D.C.

For the most part, BAA games would be played by college rules. There'd be a few differences, however. The new pro games would last 48 minutes instead of 40—a longer game would mean crowd-pleasing higher scores. And to keep the scoreboards clicking, the zone defense would be prohibited. Finally, since the games would last longer, players would be allowed six personal fouls instead of five.

As the men talked, one question kept popping up: Who would play for the new league? "We have to get the All-Americas," Ned Irish said. "We have to get George Mikan. We have to get Bob Kurland. We have to get Ernie Calverley."

Irish was right. To draw fans, the new league would have to hire the popular All-Americas who were graduating from college. But that was easier said than done. The new BAA would be competing for players with two existing leagues. One was the National Basketball League, made up of midwestern teams such as the Indianapolis Kautsky Grocers, Johnny Wooden's old team. The other was the East Coast American Basketball League, which had been dominated by the Original Celtics during the 1920s.

Before the 1946–47 season started, the BAA owners sat down to talk to Mikan, Kurland, and Calverley. "Play for us," they said, "and you can play in big arenas in New York and Chicago instead of shoebox armories in towns like Oshkosh and Trenton. That will mean higher salaries for you —much more than the two thousand dollars the other leagues have been paying."

The BAA owners were rich men. They assumed that the National and American League owners would be unable to match their high salary offers. But the BAA owners were in for a shock. The Chicago Gear Company, which owned the NBL Chicago Gears, dipped into its treasury and offered George Mikan a five-year contract for $60,-000. It was an offer Mikan couldn't refuse. To make things worse, Foothills Kurland announced that he was joining the Phillips Oil Company and would play AAU ball with the Oilers.

Not all the news was bad, however. Many of the best American League players flocked to the BAA, eager for the higher prestige— and pay—it offered. The Philadelphia Warriors signed a potential superstar named Joe Fulks. And best of all, Ernie Calverley agreed to join the new league. He would play for the Steamrollers in Providence, where his old Rhode Island fans could see him as a pro.

The BAA got off to a slow start its first season (1946–47). In New York, the Knicks played their first games in Madison

The Zollner Pistons were National Basketball League champs before joining the new BAA.

Turning pro in 1947, Ernie Calverley signed with the BAA's Providence Steamrollers.

plunge into a series of playoff games against other BAA teams. With the BAA's high salaries and short season, the owners needed these playoff games. If the playoffs drew extra-large crowds, the owners might cut their losses and at least break even.

In the first BAA playoffs, the Chicago Stags—the champs of the Western Division —upset the Caps. In the finals the Stags took on the Philadelphia Warriors, coached by the cigar-chomping Eddie Gottlieb.

The Warriors' best player was Joe Fulks, the league's high scorer. Nicknamed "Jumping Joe," Fulks was the first of the jump shooters. By now a lot of players were shooting one-handed, sometimes on the run. But

Philadelphia's Jumping Joe Fulks sinks a basket during the 1947 BAA playoffs.

Square Garden before small crowds scattered through the cavernous arena. The desperate BAA owners tried to attract more fans by scheduling double-headers. For a dollar or two, a New York fan could watch the Providence Steamrollers play the Toronto Huskies and the Knicks play the Boston Celtics. But although more than 18,000 fans clamored to get into the Garden for a college double-header featuring All-Americas such as NYU's Dolph Schayes or St. Louis's Easy Ed Macauley, barely 2,000 came to watch the pros.

Somehow, the teams managed to get through the BAA's first season. The Washington Caps finished first in the Eastern Division with a 49–11 record, the best in the league. But the Caps were not the BAA champs—far from it. Now they had to

while they always anchored one foot on the floor, the 6-foot-5 Fulks shot with both feet off the ground, popping the ball over the tallest defenders. Jumping Joe and the Warriors overwhelmed the Stags in the finals to become the first BAA champs.

It was beginning to look as if the Warriors might be the BAA's last champions, too.

After that first season, three teams dropped out of the league, and the rest all lost money. One American League team, the Baltimore Bullets, jumped to the BAA at the end of the season—but that wouldn't help the new league much.

"We don't have the stars," said Knick owner Ned Irish. "The National League has

JUMPING JOE FULKS ▪close-up▪

A cigar clenched in his teeth, Eddie Gottlieb barked into the phone. "I'll give you three thousand for the season, kid, and—"

"How much?" shouted Joe Fulks at the other end of the line in his home in Tennessee.

"I offered this hillbilly too much," Gottlieb told himself. "He's happy with three thousand. I could have gotten him for two."

In this summer of 1946, Gottlieb was trying to sign players for the Philadelphia Warriors, the team he would coach in the new BAA. Gottlieb knew that in 1943 Fulks had scored a lot of points for Murray State, a small school in Kentucky. Then Fulks had gone to the Pacific to fight the Japanese in World War II. After the war Joe had played on an army team with former All-Americas Andy Phillip and Kenny Sailors. They had raved to Gottlieb about how Fulks would suddenly stop, rise into the air, and let fly a one-hander. "It's called a jump shot," they said, "and it's impossible to block unless you're ten feet tall. He's been throwing it since high school—and he doesn't often miss."

Gottlieb wanted high scorers who would draw fans to see his team play in a new league. Now he thought he could get this hillbilly for less than three thousand.

But Joe was no innocent hillbilly. When he said "How much?" once more to Gottlieb, he made it clear that he wanted *more* money. After playing against All-Americas, he knew just how good he and his jump shot were.

Gottlieb signed Joe for almost $6,000—and got a bargain. In one of his first games in a Warrior uniform, Jumping Joe tossed in 30 points. Even the most tenacious defenders were helpless against Joe's jumper. Sometimes he'd stop with his back to the basket, corkscrew high into the air, then turn around to face the hoop and shoot. Other times he'd drive toward the basket, stop suddenly, and jump up with his legs tucked under him. Defenders would stand glued to the floor, helplessly staring as Joe let the ball fly. The jump shot's unexpectedness made it almost unstoppable.

In his first BAA season Joe scored 30 or more points in a dozen games and averaged 23 for the season. The next highest scorer in the league averaged only 16. In 1949 Jumping Joe put in 63 points in one game—a record that stood for ten years. He stayed on with the Warriors until 1954, when aching knees ended his career.

During that career, Joe was never bashful about taking shots. One year he took 400 more shots than any other player in the league. Explaining why he shot so often, Joe summed up the thoughts of all the great jump shooters who would come after him. "To win," said Jumping Joe, "you've got to have points. And you don't get points if you don't shoot."

them. We have the big arenas, but we can't fill them without the stars."

Before the 1947–48 season began, the BAA held its first draft of college All-Americas. The Chicago Stags got two All-Americas from Illinois—Andy Phillip and Gene Vance—but most college stars signed with the older National League.

The remaining BAA teams struggled through their second season. In the 1948 playoff finals, the Bullets easily took the championship away from the Warriors. The BAA had made it through another season, but its troubles weren't over yet. The BAA and the National League were still engaged in their costly bidding war for All-Americas —a war that seemed likely to destroy one or both leagues.

In the spring of 1948 Maurice Podoloff, the BAA's roly-poly commissioner, came up with an idea to save his league. He called the owners of two National League teams —the Zollners and the Kautsky Grocers— to arrange a meeting with them.

"We'll kill one another paying higher and higher salaries to these All-Americas," he told the owners. And then he made them an offer. "Join us," he said, "and your teams can play before big crowds in our large arenas."

The two National League owners jumped at the offer. Soon two other National League teams also joined the BAA. One of those teams was the Rochester Royals, led by former All-America Bob Davies. More important, the other team was the Minneapolis Lakers, which now owned the player the BAA had been seeking so long—the great George Mikan.

The National League tried to go on without Mikan, but it had lost its biggest drawing card. In the summer of 1949 the BAA agreed to take in the other National League teams. Now there were 17 teams in the league. This new, merged league was called the National Basketball Association.

The new NBA did not have one black player on its 17 teams. Although the most famous and most popular basketball team in the country was the all-black Harlem Globetrotters, many coaches and fans had considered them little more than clowns. But just before the merger, an event took place that helped change the minds of those who thought the Globies weren't good enough to play in an all-white pro league.

New York Knicks and Baltimore Bullets grapple for the ball during a 1948 game. That year the Bullets went all the way to the BAA championship.

13
Clowns or Champs?

The Minneapolis Lakers and the Harlem Globetrotters marched onto the floor of Chicago Stadium. An overflow crowd of more than 20,000 spectators filled the stands. And 5,000 more had been turned away from the game being billed as "The Rematch of the Century."

In this 1948–49 season, the Lakers were on their way to becoming the champions of the BAA. Just a few nights ago, their high scorer, the ponderous 6-foot-9 George Mikan, had dumped 53 points through the nets. He was leading the league in offense with an astounding 28 points.

Led by big George and Jim Pollard, another former All-America, the Lakers were being touted as the best pro team ever. Yet a year earlier the Lakers had been defeated in an exhibition game by the so-called "clowns" of basketball—the Harlem Globetrotters. The Globies had won that game, 61–59, on a last-second shot by Ermer Robinson.

"A lucky break," cried Laker fans, who had expected their team to steamroller over the Globetrotters. But Laker fans weren't the only ones to underestimate the Globies. In those days, many people firmly believed that blacks could not keep up with whites in a team sport like basketball, baseball, or football.

"Too dumb," the bigots said. "They don't think as fast as whites." In baseball, Jackie Robinson was already proving them wrong on the basepaths. And in football, a clever black safetyman named Emlen Tunnell was making a name for himself by outthinking quarterbacks and plucking off their passes. But so far, not one black was playing basketball in any of the organized pro leagues.

Even after the Globies' upset victory over the Lakers, few people took the Globetrotters seriously. True, the Globies were basketball's winningest team. (In one stretch they'd won over a hundred games in a row.) But whom had they beaten? A bunch of patsies who stood around while the Globies distracted them with comic antics, then sneaked to the hoop for easy baskets.

Expecting certain victory in their first confrontation with the Globetrotters, the Lakers had felt humiliated by their defeat. And now, in this 1949 rematch, they were looking for revenge. There'd be no fun and games for the Globies this time, the Lakers vowed.

Despite some serious shooting by Laker George Mikan, the Globies got the last laugh in this 1948 exhibition game.

The big rematch began, and the determined Lakers immediately took the lead. They were ahead 13–9 at the quarter and 24–18 at the half. But George Mikan wasn't pouring in his usual stream of points. The Globetrotters' young center, Nat "Sweetwater" Clifton, seemed to have a lasso around the Laker giant.

In the second half, two Globetrotter stars, Goose Tatum and Marques Haynes, suddenly got hot, and the Trotters streaked off 12 straight points. By the end of the third quarter, the score was 41–32, Globies.

Comfortably ahead, the Globies decided it was time to go into their act. A Globetrotter showed Mikan the ball, then whisked it away to a teammate. "Now you see it," the Globie chortled. "And now you don't!"

Mikan spun frantically, looking for the ball. He heard the crowd roar and suddenly knew where it was. A Globie had placed it on top of his head!

Even with their clowning, the Globies won the game, 49–45. For the second straight time, the best black team had beaten the best white team. This time there could be no doubt—blacks could play this game at least as well as whites. After the NBA was formed later that year, more and more fans demanded to know why there were no black players in the league.

By 1950 two black players had joined NBA teams. The former Globetrotter Sweetwater Clifton was playing for the New York Knicks. And Chuck Cooper, an All-America from Duquesne, was with the Boston Celtics. But NBA owners tried to keep the number of blacks on their teams to a minimum. They claimed that if they hired too many blacks, white fans would stay away from the games. They seemed to have suddenly forgotten the team that had drawn the most fans over the years—the all-black Harlem Globetrotters.

This secret NBA quota system limited teams to no more than two or three black players each. But not for long.

52

Playing for the Knicks in 1950, Sweetwater Clifton was one of only two blacks in the NBA.

14

Fierce Wildcats and Eager Beavers

Kentucky's 6-foot-8 Alex Groza caught the pass. Feinting left, then right, he wheeled out of the pivot and flipped up a hook shot. As the ball swished through the nets, the huge crowd in the Seattle arena gave Groza a standing ovation.

In this 1949 NCAA championship game between the Kentucky Wildcats and the Oklahoma Aggies, Groza had tossed in 25 points, high for both teams. Moments later, pandemonium broke out in the big arena as the Wildcats left the floor with a 46–39 victory—and their second NCAA championship in two years.

By 1949 Americans were cheering at college basketball games with the same fervor they'd once reserved for major-league baseball and college football games. (Like pro basketball teams, pro football teams played to sparse crowds.) Big-city arenas echoed with the sounds of students, alumni, and fans shrieking for their heroes. When college teams traveled, fans at home stayed glued to their radios, listening to the games.

Basketball's All-Americas were national heroes now. Youngsters all over the country yearned to play like Utah's 5-foot-7 Wat Misaka, whose stolen passes and blocked shots had led his team to the 1947 NIT championship. Little boys copied the behind-the-back dribbles of Bob Cousy, the great All-America from Holy Cross. And in countless high school gyms other boys tried to loop in one-handed jump shots like the University of Southern California's Bill Sharman.

But no basketball players were more famous than the University of Kentucky's Alex Groza, Ralph Beard, and Wallace "Wah Wah" Jones. The willowy 6-foot-8 Groza outleaped the tallest centers, and he

Kentucky's Alex Groza gets a boost from his happy teammates after the 1949 NCAA finals.

had the speed and stamina to run them ragged. The 6-foot-5 Wah Wah Jones zigzagged around forwards with lightning-bolt dashes to the hoop. And like a cannonball, six-foot Ralph Beard blasted through defenses for his driving lay-ups.

Coached by Kentucky's Adolph Rupp, these three players had led the Wildcats to a 32–1 record and the NCAA title during the 1948–49 season. When the United Press selected its five-man All-America team that year, three of the five—Groza, Beard, and Jones—were Wildcats. "This," said the former Celtic Joe Lapchick, "is the greatest team ever—college or pro."

With the 1949 NCAA crown on their heads, the Kentucky Wildcats flew to New York for the NIT at Madison Square Garden. If the Wildcats could win here, they would become the first team in basketball history to capture the double crown—the NCAA and NIT championships—in one year.

But the Wildcats went home to Kentucky with only the NCAA trophy. In the opening round of the NIT, they were upset, 61–56, by a scrappy team of unknowns from Loyola. (Loyola fought all the way to the finals before being edged out of the championship, 48–47, by the University of San Francisco.) Groza, Beard, and Jones graduated without savoring the double triumph that a ragged "Cinderella" team—not an All-America on it—would come out of nowhere to win in 1950.

Millions of dollars had been bet on the 1949 NIT. Newspapers printed the "point

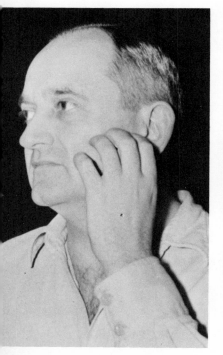

ADOLPH RUPP ▪ close-up ▪

"I know I have plenty of enemies," Kentucky coach Adolph Rupp once said. "But I'd rather be the most hated coach in the country than the most popular one. Show me a popular coach, and I'll show you a loser."

Loud and argumentative with referees, reporters, fans, and players, the imperious Rupp (nicknamed "The Baron") never won any popularity contests. But in his 43 years as a college coach, he and his teams won just about everything else. From 1944 to 1952 Kentucky won the southeastern conference championship nine times in a row. Fifteen of his teams qualified for the NCAA tournament, a record that still stood when he retired in the '70s. And four of those teams won the championship. Overall, Rupp's Wildcats won more than eight of every ten games they played.

During the 1930s and '40s, there were a number of outstanding college coaches—Hank Iba (Oklahoma A & M), Phog Allen (Kansas), Clair Bee (LIU), George Keogan (Notre Dame), Branch McCracken (Indiana), Frank Keaney (Rhode Island State), Nat Holman (CCNY), and Joe Lapchick (St. John's). But none was more colorful, controversial, or successful than the Baron.

Born on a Kansas farm in 1901, Rupp played for Phog Allen on the 1922 and 1923 Kansas teams that were acclaimed national champions. In 1930 he became head coach at Kentucky. At that time many young men from the South and the West believed that basketball, with its rules against body contact, was a sissy sport for pale city boys. Country boys liked the ruggedness of football.

Adolph Rupp rounded up strong country boys and cajoled them into playing basketball. He lashed them through hours of drills until he had molded them into a smooth scoring machine.

One day a Kentucky player told Rupp that he had just finished practicing his free throws. "How many did you put in?" asked Rupp.

"Twenty-three of twenty-five," the player said proudly.

"What happened to the other two?" growled the Baron.

Throughout his career, the Baron stressed discipline and hard work. His players may not always have liked Rupp's coaching methods, but they couldn't argue with his results.

Kentucky's Ralph Beard and Loyola's Jim Nicholl chase a loose ball in the 1949 NIT.

heavier in the 1949–50 season as an underdog team, Nat Holman's CCNY Beavers, knocked over one favorite after another to reach the finals of the NIT.

In the finals, the Beavers opposed a fast-breaking team from Bradley, led by All-America Gene "Squeaky" Melchiorre. Bradley was ranked the number one college team in the nation, while CCNY wasn't even in the top ten. The Beaver starters were mostly sophomores and juniors. The only veteran was a not-too-quick Irwin Dambrot. Their center, Ed Roman, stood just 6-foot-5. And the other players—Floyd Layne and Ed Warner among them—were typical New York give-and-go players.

Bradley was clearly the favorite. But then the Beavers hadn't been favored against third-ranked Kentucky or sixth-ranked Duquesne—and those were the teams they'd eliminated on their way to the finals.

CCNY's Ed Warner drives to the basket in the 1950 NIT vs. Duquesne.

spread" for college games—Kentucky, for example, had been favored to beat Loyola by ten points. That meant that if you bet on Kentucky, the Wildcats had to win by more than ten points or you lost your bet with the bookmaker. But if you bet on Loyola, you could collect even if Loyola *lost*—as long as they didn't lose by more than ten points.

The "spread" was what made betting on basketball so exciting and popular. You could bet on the underdog and have as good a chance of winning as if you had bet on the favorite. (The point spreads were made up carefully by experts to balance the teams evenly.) And the betting grew even

With the Bradley Braves favored to win the championship by six or seven points, an entire nation of fans tuned in their radios and televisions to see if CCNY could win the big game. And the Beavers didn't disappoint their fans. While cheerleaders urged them on with CCNY's catchy "Allagaroo" cheer, the Beavers captured the NIT crown with a 69–61 victory.

A week later Holman and his Cinderella team plunged into the NCAA eastern regionals, which were held at the Garden. CCNY outplayed second-ranked Ohio State and fifth-ranked North Carolina State to reach the finals.

In the finals CCNY again faced Bradley.

This time the score was closer, but CCNY hung on to win, 71–68, and become the first—and last—team ever to win both the NCAA and NIT championships.

Perched on the shoulders of his jubilant players, coach Nat Holman hugged CCNY's second championship trophy in a week. Already he was looking forward to the next season when his young Beavers seemed destined to snatch the "greatest-ever" accolade from Adolph Rupp's 1948–49 Kentucky Wildcats. The happy coach had no way of knowing that before the next year ended, he and his players would be buffeted by a scandal that rocked basketball and shocked the nation.

15

Scandal!

Standing on the sidelines, CCNY coach Nat Holman formed a T with his hands. His players saw the signal and called a time-out. As the CCNY Beavers gathered around him, Nat grabbed one of his players. The gray-haired coach had to raise his voice to be heard above the din that rocked Madison Square Garden during this 1950 game. "Look," Nat shouted at the player, "you must stand in *front* of that pivotman and block him off from the ball. When he gets that ball, he kills us."

The player nodded. But when the game resumed, he took the same position—*behind* the opposing pivotman. Nat frowned as the ball was bounced in to the pivotman, who swung toward the basket and dropped in an uncontested shot.

CCNY won the game, but the incident made Nat wonder. Had his player been giving his best? By the 1950–51 season, it was being whispered around New York that gamblers had bribed some college stars not to play all out. According to the rumors, players were given money to "dump" a

game—that is, to lose it deliberately. Other players, it was said, were bribed to "shave" points—that is, to purposely win a game by only a few points (to beat the point spread) when a greater margin of victory was possible.

Nat Holman couldn't believe the talk, certainly not about his team. After all, CCNY had won both the NCAA and NIT trophies in 1950. And in the early part of the 1950–51 season, his young Beavers had mowed down one opponent after another. By January 1951, the team was being compared to that "greatest of all teams," the 1948–49 Kentucky Wildcats. But as Holman soon discovered, the rumors were true.

Early in 1951 a gangling Manhattan College player named Junius Kellogg sat down in the office of the Manhattan district attorney. He told the D.A. that he had been offered a bribe to shave points. After refusing the bribe, he had come directly to the D.A.

An investigation began immediately. Before it ended a year later, the police and

Junius Kellogg of CCNY meets the press after breaking the college basketball scandal to a Manhattan district attorney.

the FBI had uncovered a hornet's nest. Between 1947 and 1950, it was found, players in more than 80 college games had accepted money to shave points or dump games. And the players involved included some of the biggest stars in the nation. Kentucky's Ralph Beard and Alex Groza had taken money to shave points against Loyola in the 1949 NIT. (In fact, they had shaved so finely that they unintentionally lost.) Other big names implicated in the scandal were Floyd Layne and Ed Roman of the champion

Players implicated in the point-shaving scandal included Bradley's Gene Melchiorre, Kentucky's Ralph Beard, and LIU's Sherman White (from left to right).

CCNY team, Bradley's Gene Melchiorre, LIU's Sherman White, and dozens more from the nation's powerhouses.

The guilty players were expelled from school and banned from the NBA. Although many fans felt that the players had gotten off easy, to the athletes involved, the punishment was devastating. For most of these players, basketball was much more than a game. It was a way of life.

"I thought I would be all right once I was too old to play basketball," Ralph Beard said many years later. "But I'm forty-six now, and it still hurts. I'll never get over it until I die."

Floyd Layne began to teach neighborhood youngsters how to play basketball. One of his first pupils, in a black ghetto in the Bronx, was a scrawny boy named Nate Archibald. By 1975 Layne had come all the way back to become the head basketball coach at CCNY. "I came up from the pit," he said, "I can't tell you how good I feel."

The basketball scandal affected all players—even those who were completely innocent. Basketball fans were horrified by the disclosures. "How can you be sure a game or a player is honest?" they said. "How do we know about those kids who are still playing? They could still be shaving points."

Embarrassed by the scandal, red-faced college presidents tried to put the blame solely on the professional gamblers who hung around big-city arenas tempting the young athletes. The college officials knew they couldn't keep the gamblers out of the arenas, so they decided to take their players away. College teams went back to playing most of their games in campus gyms.

No longer did fans swarm into the Garden and other arenas to see the NIT and college double-headers. Nor did they follow the All-Americas to their campus field houses. Instead, basketball fans began to look for new heroes. And they found them—in the new NBA.

16

The Mikan Era

A long line of fans straggled out onto Manhattan's Eighth Avenue one winter evening in 1954. The fans were lined up to buy tickets to a basketball game at Madison Square Garden. But unlike the Garden crowd of the late 1940s, these fans were waiting to buy tickets to a pro basketball game. And the marquee over Madison Square Garden explained why so many had been drawn here. In big black letters it read: "TONIGHT—THE KNICKS VS. GEORGE MIKAN."

George Mikan drew crowds wherever he and his team, the Minneapolis Lakers, came to play. The 6-foot-9 giant was the most awesome scorer of the day. In 1948–49 he and the Lakers had joined what soon became the NBA. Immediately George had grabbed the league lead in scoring, dropping in 28 points a game to pull ahead of Jumping Joe Fulks's 26. Not surprisingly, the Lakers had romped to the 1948–49 league championship.

The following season, Minneapolis won the championship for the second year in a row. And again the 6-foot-9, 240-pound George led the league in scoring.

But the Lakers were no one-man team. Flanking George were two of basketball's most powerful forwards—the 6-foot-8 Vern Mikkelsen and the 6-foot-5 Jim Pollard. Standing shoulder to shoulder, Mikan, Mikkelsen, and Pollard looked like a jagged row of Alpine mountains. Smaller opponents were simply overwhelmed when the three big Lakers grabbed rebounds or tapped in shots.

The Laker attack was as basic as a punch in the nose. When an opposing player's shot hopped off the rim, one of the Lakers' three big men would reach up and snatch it. Most

likely, the ball would then be tossed to Slater Martin, the Lakers' slick ballhandler. The 5-foot-9 Martin would dribble the ball leisurely over the midcourt line while big George lumbered toward the hoop. "Wait for George!" became the Laker battle cry.

George would anchor himself in the pivot position. If only one man was trying to contain the mammoth Mikan, Martin would lob the ball over to George. Elbows flying as he mowed a path to the basket, Mikan would whirl and drop in a hook shot.

But Mikan was rarely guarded by just one defender. Most teams tried to gang up on the big Laker. Two—sometimes three—players would kick his legs and poke their elbows into his ribs. But when players

George Mikan outscrambles two New York Knicks for the ball.

ganged up on Mikan, Martin simply flashed the ball to Pollard or Mikkelsen. Big and fast, each could loop in 20 or 30 points if Mikan was ringed by opponents.

In 1950–51 Mikan led the league in scoring for the third straight year—and Mikan and Co. aimed for their third straight NBA championship. But the Rochester Royals upset the Lakers in the playoffs and won the championship.

After the game, Mikan confidently told his Laker teammates, "We'll win that cham-pionship again." The following season (1951–52) fans streamed into arenas to see if Mikan and Co. could retrieve the NBA championship from Rochester. And the crowd swelled as thousands of disillusioned fans turned their backs on the scandal-ridden college game.

Now basketball began to mean *pro* bas-ketball. A TV network telecast NBA games each Saturday afternoon, giving millions of people across the nation their first view of the slam-bang physical fury of the pro

GEORGE MIKAN ▪close-up▪

Fifteen-year-old George Mikan clutched the ball. As he swung his body to pivot for a hook shot, a player accidentally kicked his right leg. George col-lapsed, the leg broken. Before a doctor could set the fracture, an infection set in.

For 18 months in 1939 and 1940, George lay on a bed in his room while the leg healed. When he finally got out of the bed to totter out of the room, he had to stoop to pass through the doorway. He had grown from 5-foot-11 to 6-foot-7.

Now he towered above his classmates at Quigley Prep in Chicago. The basketball coach asked him to play center, and George agreed. George clearly had a height advantage over his opponents, but his sudden growth had made him awkward. When he turned to the basket, the gangling youngster often tripped over his own feet.

George wanted to be a lawyer, not a basketball player. But he knew his parents couldn't afford the expense of college and law school. He tried out for the Notre Dame team, hoping to win a scholarship. But after watching George, the Notre Dame coach turned to his assistant, Ray Meyer, and said: "He's too awkward—and besides he wears glasses."

A dejected George slouched out of the gym, ashamed of his great height. A few months later, however, Ray Meyer became the head coach at DePaul University and offered George an athletic scholarship there. Meyer ordered the gawky freshman to skip rope and shadow box. He also told George to scrimmage one-on-one against a catlike 5-foot-6 guard. And as George became more agile, Meyer had him practice a sweeping hook shot by the hour.

"As soon as George stopped feeling sorry for himself and realized his height was something to be admired," Meyer once said, "he was on his way to being great."

All of George's hard work paid off. The high-scoring center won All-America recognition three straight years and was twice acclaimed the college player of the year. When he graduated in 1946, George joined the Chicago Gears of the National Basketball League.

Hardened pros waited with clenched fists to cut the giant rookie down to size. The first time George put on a Chicago uniform, an opposing center knocked out four of his teeth. Bleeding from the mouth, George stayed in the game. The violence made the college game seem like kid stuff. The huge pros, bigger than football fullbacks, cracked into each other—and without any pads to protect them. And in the pro game (unlike college ball) the referee's whistle rarely stopped the action when players collided.

Pro ball was fast and exciting—and totally unpredictable. Games were often undecided until the final seconds. Leads seesawed back and forth. First one team was ahead by ten; then the other team made a rush and caught up. Leads as large as 15 points vanished in minutes. Pro sharpshooters such as Mikan, Boston's Bob Cousy, and Rochester's Bob Davies sent a steady stream of basketballs through the hoop.

Basketball fans had never seen such an array of shooters on one floor until they saw their first NBA game. In any given contest, most of the ten players on the floor were likely to be former All-Americas. And any one of them could score 20 or 30 points

game and contributed 25 points to the Gears' victory.

After the Gears folded, George was picked up by the Minneapolis Lakers. In five seasons (from 1949–50 to 1953–54) he led the Lakers to four NBA titles. And for two of those seasons George was the NBA's top scorer, tossing a steady stream of hook shots from around the hoop.

Trying to stop Mikan as he wheeled out of the pivot spot was like stepping into the path of a bulldozer. His eyeglasses glinting, Mikan swung shoulders and elbows to mow a path to the basket. After one particularly rough game, a rival accused Mikan of being a dirty player. Mikan tore off his shirt and pointed to the black-and-blue marks that covered his chest. "What do you think these are," he snapped, "birthmarks?"

With so many rivals determined to keep him away from the hoop, Mikan had to be tough. It was a matter of self-defense. "You've got to give it right back to them with a basket or a punch," George once said, "or they'll pound you right out of the league."

Opposing players weren't the only ones who tried to stop Mikan. The big man was such a dominating force on offense that NBA officials feared the fans would get bored watching his one-man scoring show. To give the smaller players a chance, the officials agreed to expand the foul lane from 6 to 12 feet. Since an offensive player could stand in the lane only three seconds, Mikan had to take more outside shots—from at least 12 feet away. The rule became known as the "Mikan Rule," but it didn't stop George. Although his scoring average dropped several points as a result of it, Mikan continued to be one of the league's highest scorers.

In 1950 George Mikan was picked as the greatest basketball player of the first half-century. In 1954 he retired to become a lawyer (he later became commissioner of the American Basketball Association). After Mikan retired, the pro game became much faster. Some fans claimed that the plodding George would have been left behind by the flashy pro centers of the 1960s and '70s. But Red Auerbach, the old Boston Celtic coach, disagreed. "George Mikan," he said, "had the determination and courage to be the best, no matter who or what tried to stop him. He would have been a standout in any era."

In 1953 Mikan & Co. celebrate another championship—the Lakers' fourth in five years.

in a game. The new jump shooters were the most spectacular. Leaping higher than Jumping Joe Fulks—and hanging in the air even longer—was a Philadelphia Warrior named Paul Arizin. "He goes up into the air like he was climbing a ladder," an opponent said of Arizin. "Then he just seems to sit there and plop the ball into the hoop."

All these supershooters gave George and the Lakers some stiff competition. In 1951–52 Arizin beat Mikan out of the league scoring crown, and the Lakers finished second in the West behind the defending champions, the Rochester Royals. But in the playoffs George and the Lakers rose up to vanquish Rochester in the semi-finals. Then they met the Knicks in the finals. In seven tense, seesawing games, the Lakers captured the 1952 NBA title—their third championship in four years.

Mikan and Co. went on winning—and drawing big crowds. But not everyone who came to watch big George could be called a fan. "Everybody roots against the big

man," Mikan once explained. "Wherever we play, people hope the hometown team will beat us. We usually win, but the people come back again hoping that the next time we'll take a fall."

But those who hoped to see the Lakers' dynasty topple were disappointed. The Lakers won the NBA championship in 1953 and again in 1954. They had ruled the league for three straight years and for five of the six years they had been in the NBA. "This is the greatest team in history," said NBA commissioner Maurice Podoloff. "And George Mikan is the greatest player ever."

At the end of that 1953–54 season, the 30-year-old Mikan announced his retirement. NBA owners winced when they heard that George would not be around for the 1954–55 season. Ever since the birth of the NBA in 1949, Mikan had been the league's number one drawing card. Now, in 1954, many of the league's teams were still unsteady on their feet—and without the steadying hand of big George, it was feared they might stumble and fall.

17

Biasone Brings the Clock

With only 50 seconds remaining in this 1954 NBA game, the Boston Celtics led the Philadelphia Warriors by one point. Celtic coach Red Auerbach signaled for a time-out. As his players gathered around him, Auerbach turned to a slender dark-haired guard named Bob Cousy. "Bob," he said, "see if you can dribble out the clock."

The game resumed, and the ball was passed to Cousy. He immediately started to dribble along the center line, bouncing the ball behind his back and between his legs. Several pairs of Warrior hands reached out for the ball, but no one could bat it away from Cousy. Finally, a desperate Warrior whacked Bob across the arms. It was an intentional foul. The Warriors knew Cousy would be given one free throw. But then the Warriors would get the ball and a chance to sink a fast two-point basket.

As expected, Cousy dropped in his free throw. But the Warriors' hasty shot missed its mark. Now the Celtics had the ball—and a two-point lead. Again the ball was passed to Cousy. And again he tried to run out the clock with his fancy dribbling. The Philadelphia fans began to boo. As long as Cousy monopolized the ball, the Warriors couldn't even hope to tie up the game. But Cousy kept right on dribbling. Now only 20 seconds remained. The Warriors had to give another intentional foul to get the ball. Again Cousy dropped in the free throw.

The Celtics won the game by three points and left a jeering crowd behind them in the arena. Later, Warrior coach Eddie Gottlieb puffed angrily on a cigar as he talked to reporters. "Sure, Cousy's great," he snarled. "He can freeze the ball. But I doubt whether freezing helps the league."

By 1954 more and more teams were re-

A master ballhandler, Boston's Bob Cousy dribbles out the clock.

lying on the last-minute freeze to win close games. As coach Auerbach explained, "All that dribbling, and those clutch-and-grab fouls plus those long walks to the foul lines may be dull to fans. But the fans expect us to win. And if you freeze the ball when you're ahead, the other team can't score. There's no way you can lose."

Auerbach was right—the fans did want to see their teams win. But they also wanted to see an exciting game. And even the most avid fans were bored by the endless dribbling and free-throw shooting that delayed the endings of so many games. The ending of one 1954 playoff game dragged on so long that the TV network cut the game off the

63

air, even though one team led by only a point.

The NBA couldn't afford to lose any of its fans—especially the television viewers. The league needed the sums of money it received from the TV network that broadcast the games. Although attendance at the pro games in 1954 was higher than ever, so were player salaries and the teams' other operating expenses. Of the 17 teams that had been members of the NBA in 1949, only nine were still in business by the start of the 1954–55 season.

At their annual meeting in 1954, the owners discussed the problem. "We've lost Mikan, our number one drawing attraction," one owner said. "We've got to do something to make the game more appealing to fans and TV viewers."

Another owner, Syracuse's Danny Biasone, thought he knew how to make the game faster and more exciting. He suggested a new rule that would compel a team to shoot the ball within 24 seconds. If a team didn't get off a shot within that time, it would have to hand the ball over to its opponents. The 24-second rule would make it impossible for a team to freeze the ball.

"Why twenty-four seconds?" one owner asked.

As Danny explained it, in a typical NBA game, each team fired an average of 120 shots—one every 24 seconds. If teams were required to shoot within 24 seconds, they couldn't complain about being rushed into doing what they had been doing on their own.

The owners agreed to try Danny's 24-second rule. They also borrowed a rule from the college game to discourage intentional fouls. Now each team would be limited to six fouls per quarter. If a team went over the limit, its opponent would get a "bonus" foul shot.

With this bonus rule, it would no longer make sense to foul intentionally in the hope of giving a one-point free throw in exchange

Danny Biasone originated the 24-second rule and revolutionized the game.

for a two-point basket. Now a deliberate foul could cost a team two points.

When the 1954–55 season began, the 24-second clocks were stationed along the sidelines of every NBA arena. Overnight, the pro game changed. With teams taking more shots, scores soared higher and higher—past the 100-point mark in many games. Fans were delighted with basketball's fast new pace, and a bigger TV network bid to televise the games.

During that season Baltimore dropped out of the league. The NBA was reduced to eight teams—Boston, New York, Philadelphia, and Syracuse in the East; Fort Wayne, Milwaukee, Minneapolis, and Rochester in the West. In the next 20 years after Danny Biasone brought his clock to the pros, teams would move from one city to another—but not a single NBA team would go out of business.

18

The Key to a Championship

"The big guy is gone."

Those words echoed through NBA dressing rooms at the start of the 1954–55 season. The NBA owners may have missed George Mikan, but the players certainly didn't. Now that the elbow-swinging Mikan had retired, teeth would be a lot safer under NBA backboards. And now other NBA teams would finally get a crack at the league championship, which had been monopolized by the Lakers for three straight years.

Many people assumed that the Philadelphia Warriors would be the first team to dethrone the Mikan-less Lakers. The Warriors had a supercenter of their own— 6-foot-9 Neil Johnston. The strong, long-armed Johnston could arch the ball over the head of an opponent and drop it into the basket with the ease of a man hanging up his hat. Johnston led the NBA in scoring with 23 points a game. And the league's number

Warrior supercenter Neil Johnston gets off a shot against the St. Louis Hawks.

two scorer was another Warrior—Paul Arizin, who averaged 20 points a game. Yet even with such fine talent, the Warriors finished a surprising dead-last in their division.

Led by 6-foot-7 Dolph Schayes, the Syracuse Nats streaked to first place in the NBA East Division, and the Fort Wayne Pistons won in the West. When the two teams met in the finals, it was clear that they were evenly matched. They scrapped through the first six games, each winning three. The seventh and final game went right down to the wire, the lead seesawing back and forth all night. With only 12 seconds remaining, the teams were deadlocked, 91–91. Then Syracuse's George King dropped in a free throw, and the Nats became the new NBA champions.

The Nats weren't champs for long, however. The Warriors came back in 1955–56 determined to win the NBA championship. This time, the Warriors had a new name on their roster—Tom Gola, a 6-foot-5 All-America from LaSalle.

With Gola at forward, Philadelphia looked like a new team. Gola was a fine shooter, but the Warriors already had plenty of high scorers. What they needed was a good rebounder, and Gola quickly proved he was one of the best. A strong, burly forward, he grabbed rebounds left and right, then fed the ball to Johnston and Arizin. With Gola taking care of the rebounding, the high-scoring Warriors got off more shots than ever. They finished first in the East, then stormed past the Fort Wayne Pistons to win the '56 championship.

In one short season, the Warriors had gone from last place all the way to the league championship. And the key to their success had been the fine rebounding of Tom Gola. Other teams witnessed the Warriors' instant turnaround and began looking for strong rebounders of their own.

"We need someone like Gola," said Boston Celtic coach Red Auerbach, whose team

had been eliminated in the first round of the 1956 playoffs. "You have to get the ball to score. I have the shooters who can score. But I don't have someone to grab those rebounds and feed the ball to my shooters."

No one could deny that the Celtics had the shooters. At guard was Bill Sharman, who threw in more jumpers than anyone except Arizin. And when it came to shooting fouls, Sharman was second to no one. He had once looped in 50 free throws in a row. At center was Easy Ed Macauley, who dipped in soft hook shots. And then there was Bob Cousy. A former All-America guard from Holy Cross, Cousy was a master ballhandler and a supershooter. Almost every season he led the Celtics in scoring

The happy Philadelphia Warriors celebrate their 1956 NBA championship.

with 20 or more points a game. And almost every season he led the NBA in assists.

Yet despite all the points being piled up by Cousy, Sharman, and Macauley, the Celtics never got very far in the playoffs. "Before the 24-second clock," said Auerbach, "a team could win almost anytime it scored 100 points. But now, with everyone taking more shots, you usually have to score 105 or 110 points to win. And we don't get the ball to our scorers often enough to score that many points."

Auerbach set out to search for a center who could leap high enough to pull down rebounds and feed the ball to the Boston sharpshooters. Before the 1956–57 season began, Auerbach would find his rebounder. And that rebounder would go on to become one of the greatest all-around players in the history of pro basketball.

19

Point Fever

By the 1950s basketball was being watched —and played—by more Americans than any other team sport. The NBA had introduced millions of fans to the excitement of basketball. But some of the game's most avid fans had never even seen a big-league game. In every state from coast to coast these fans gathered in tiny gyms to cheer on their local grade school, high school, or college teams. And nowhere were the cheers louder than in the state of Indiana.

Ever since Johnny Wooden's days as a star for Martinsville High, Indiana fans had turned out in droves to watch their teams battle through the state's high school championship tournament. "Hysteria is another name for Indiana basketball at tournament time," someone once said. That was true in Wooden's day, and it's still true today. But no Indiana final generated more hysteria than the one in 1954.

Matched against Muncie Central, one of the biggest schools in the state, was Milan High School, which had only 73 male students. Fortunately, for Milan, one of the 73 was a 5-foot-10 sharpshooter named Bobby Plump. That season Plump tossed in enough points to catapult little Milan past much bigger schools into this final.

As the game began, some 18,000 screaming people (more than ten times the popula-

tion of the town of Milan) packed the arena at Butler Field House in Indianapolis. Cool and poised, Bobby and his teammates ignored the drum-banging din around them and concentrated on the business at hand. For three periods they matched the boys from Muncie point for point. Midway through the fourth period Muncie led, 28–26, but Milan's Bobby Plump had the ball. Bobby dribbled across the midline, then stuck the ball under his arm and held it there for more than five minutes. The Muncie Central fans began to jeer. But the five panting Milan players were exhausted after trying to keep up with the waves of fresh players that came off the Muncie bench. Little Milan was lucky to have five starters, and substitutes were a luxury they couldn't afford. Bobby and his teammates wanted to save their energy for a final burst.

With about a minute to go, Milan came alive. Bobby tossed the ball to a teammate who tied up the game, 28–all, with a quick two-pointer. The Muncie players responded with a basket of their own, but Milan came right back to tie it up again. Muncie tried to regain the lead with another basket, but the ball hit the rim and bounced off.

With only eight seconds of play remaining, one of the Milan boys leaped up and snatched the rebound. He passed the ball to Bobby Plump. Precious seconds ticked away as Bobby dribbled through a forest of Muncie players. Near the keyhole he braked, rose in the air, and floated a one-hander toward the hoop. Almost simultaneously, the ball splashed through the nets and the final buzzer sounded. There was a split second of total silence, and then the huge crowd let out a mighty roar. In the greatest upset in the history of Indiana basketball, little Milan High School had won the state championship.

In small towns all over America, crowds roared just as enthusiastically at college games. Many of these colleges were so small that few people living more than 50 miles away had ever heard of them. And one of the smallest was Rio Grande College in Ohio. Yet for a few years Rio Grande became one of the best-known schools in the nation.

It all started one day in 1954 when a 6-foot-9 freshman named Clarence "Bevo" Francis floated in a record-shattering 113 points in one game, as his Rio Grande team buried an opponent 150–40. Big-city newspaper reporters immediately flocked to the little college town to find out what was going on.

The reporters learned that Rio Grande had few students and almost no money. In 1953 the basketball coach, Newt Oliver, had decided that if his team could score its way to fame, it would draw enough paying fans to fill the treasury with money. With a total student body of only 95, Rio Grande didn't have much of a team. But that didn't stop Oliver. He simply borrowed $3,000 and set out to build a team. He handed out scholarships—and promises of instant fame —to Bevo Francis and four other good high school players.

Oliver's plan worked perfectly. In 1954 Bevo and Co. overwhelmed the competition. Playing against such teams as Bliss Business College and Cincinnati Seminary, the boys from Rio Grande were just about unbeat-

The super scoring of Bevo Francis put little Rio Grande College on the map.

able. In one game Bevo slammed in 150 points to lead his team to a 210–35 rout. Bevo's points were like money in the bank for Rio Grande. The team played to standing-room-only crowds, and the school began to prosper.

Rio Grande slipped back to obscurity in 1955 after Bevo quit school to play for a touring pro team, coached by Newt Oliver. Bevo never made it to the NBA, and his pro career was short and undistinguished. But some two decades after he set them, Bevo Francis's scoring records were still on the books.

Francis was only one of a host of college

players who brought new excitement to the game of basketball in the years following the 1951 point-shaving scandal. In 1952 Kansas coach Phog Allen saw his 6-foot-9 Clyde "Man Mountain" Lovellette drop in an average of 28 points a game. (That was more points than Phog's entire team had scored in many 1930s games.) During his outstanding college career Lovellette whisked in 1,888 points, more than any player before him. But that record didn't last long. A year later Seattle's Johnny O'Brien demolished it with a total of 2,537. A Furman player named Frank Selvy slammed in 100 points in a single game, racked up 50 or more in eight others, and averaged 32 per game that year—a major-college record. And the whole Furman team set another record by averaging 90 points a game, better than double the old point-a-minute standard.

Yet even as scoreboards blinked off higher and higher numbers, many coaches were becoming convinced that a team could not win with points alone. Winning teams had to play a gluey defense, they claimed. Coming along was a player who would bring as much excitement to the art of defense as Francis, Lovellette, and Selvy had brought to offense. In 1951 he was the third-string center at a small high school in California. But within a decade he'd become the greatest center in the NBA. His name was William Felton Russell.

Sharp-shooting collegians Clyde Lovellette (left) of Kansas and Frank Selvy (right) of Furman set new scoring records during the 1950s.

20
Big Bill

Coach George Powles had to crane his neck to stare up at the tall, skinny student before him. On this fall day in 1949 the coach had seen the gangling youth slouching along a corridor at McClymonds High School in Oakland, California. Powles had run up to him and caught his arm. "You're a big fellow," the coach said. "Why don't you come out for the basketball team?"

Young Bill Russell shifted his eyes. "Other fellows are better than I am," he mumbled shyly.

"Son, remember this," the coach said. "If you think the other guy is better than you are, he will be."

Bill smiled ruefully. That was easy for the coach to say. He didn't know how unco-ordinated Bill was. The 6-foot-6 Russell had already tried out for—and been turned down by—the homeroom basketball team, the football team, and even the cheerleading squad. Bill had just about given up. "I'm too awkward for sports," he told Powles.

The coach wouldn't take no for an answer, however, so Bill finally agreed to try out for the team. As soon as Russell got on the court, it was clear that he was awkward. He flubbed passes, slipped, and stumbled. Powles watched the clumsy youngster for a few minutes and then motioned him over to the sidelines. "You've got to smooth out your moves," he told Bill kindly. "We'll put you on the junior varsity."

Bill was the 16th player on a JV team that had only 15 uniforms. He and another player shared a uniform—Bill would wear it for one game, his teammate would wear it for the next.

But even when he was in uniform, Russell rarely got to play. He just wasn't good enough. The only times he saw any action were in the final minutes of a game when the JV was so far ahead—or behind—that the outcome was already assured. Then the McClymonds students would chant derisively, "We want Russell!" When Bill came into the game, the fans would laugh as he tripped over his own feet and tossed up hook shots that sailed high over the backboard.

But Russell was determined to become a real basketball player. He worked hard, and his hours of practice began to pay off. Late in his junior year (1950–51) he was promoted to the varsity. He was only the team's third-string center, but that didn't bother Bill. "At least I have my own uniform," he told a friend.

Now Bill stood 6-foot-8, and he was becoming an incredible leaper. He could soar high enough to place a coin on the top of a backboard. Bill still wasn't much of a shooter, but he was fast becoming a superior defenseman. With his kangaroo leaps and bounds, he easily blocked the shots of his tallest rivals.

Russell's amazing shot-blocking ability earned him the starting slot at center in his senior year. He did a fine job all season. In March 1952, McClymonds met Oakland High for the city championship. That game turned out to be the most important game in Bill's high school career.

As the game began, a University of San Francisco scout slipped into his seat. He'd come here to offer a scholarship to the Oakland center, Truman Bruce. But Bruce never made it to San Francisco. Although Bruce was a fine athlete, that night he was outplayed at both ends of the court by Bill Russell. Bill scored 14 points, snared 19 rebounds, and blocked countless shots. After the game, the scout offered the scholarship to Russell.

Bill accepted eagerly. That was the first —and only—college scholarship he was ever offered. In the fall of 1952 he walked onto the University of San Francisco campus. Now a rawboned 6-foot-9 and 190 pounds, Bill felt a new sense of confidence. "I'll never be a great scorer," he told people, "but I can stop other people from being great scorers."

True to his word, Bill blocked shots left and right, and the San Francisco Dons became the nation's best defensive team. In 1953–54, Bill and the Dons allowed their opponents a mere 55 points a game. And the Dons had their first winning season (14–7) since 1950.

The next year (1954–55) the Dons won their first two games. Their third opponent was UCLA, coached by the old India Rubber Man, Johnny Wooden. Bill knew that Wooden's team never stopped running. Before the game the nervous Russell threw up. (Bill was so eager to play well that he often got sick in the locker room.) As the game began, it was clear that Bill had reason to be nervous. He was simply powerless against UCLA's high scorer, Willie Naulls. Time after time, Naulls lofted the ball over Russell's outstretched arms and into the hoop. UCLA beat San Francisco, 47–40.

"It's my fault!" cried Bill as he bolted into the dressing room after the game. "It's my fault!" The dejected Russell slumped onto a stool and bowed his head.

"It's not your fault," coach Phil Woolpert shot back. "It's everybody's fault. Forget it. We'll have another crack at UCLA next week."

Sure enough, when the Dons faced UCLA a week later, it was a whole different ball game. Bill soared to new heights, completely nullifying Naulls, and San Francisco won

His great leaping ability made Bill Russell (6) a double threat: shot-blocking on defense . . .

by 12 points. For the rest of Bill's college career, UCLA would never again defeat the Dons—nor would any other team. The Dons went on to finish that season with 26 straight victories and won the 1955 NCAA championship by defeating LaSalle, 77–63. San Francisco was ranked number one in the nation, and Bill Russell was named to every All-America team.

"Bill Russell makes us a great defensive ball club," said coach Woolpert. "He has given this game a new weapon—the blocked shot."

Russell's contributions to the Dons

. . . and slam-dunking on offense.

weren't limited solely to defense, however. On offense, the big man would station himself near the basket, wait for a pass from a teammate, then stuff the ball through the hoop. From that same position, he'd often reach up, catch a teammate's shot in mid-flight, and steer the ball into the basket. At the end of the 1954–55 season, the colleges passed a new rule aimed at giants like Bill. As the pros had done a few years earlier,

they widened the "three-second" lane near the basket from 6 to 12 feet. No longer could Russell anchor himself near the hoop for an easy lay-up.

There was no way to stop Bill on defense, however, and he went right on blocking shots. In 1955–56 the Dons were again the nation's top defensive team. This time they yielded only 52 points a game. They finished the season with an incredible 29–0 record and stretched their winning streak to 55 victories. In the NCAA finals they overwhelmed Iowa, 83–71, for their second straight NCAA championship. Again, the Dons were ranked number one, and again Russell was a unanimous choice for All-America honors.

Word of Russell's exploits spread clear across the country. Some 3,000 miles away from San Francisco, Boston Celtic coach Red Auerbach was still looking for a good leaper who could seize rebounds and feed the ball to his high scorers. He heard about Bill Russell and asked a scout to tell him more.

"He can't hit the side of a barn when he's more than fifteen feet from the basket," the scout said. "And he's so skinny that bigger centers shove him around under the hoop. But he is the best basketball player I have ever seen."

"How can that be?" Auerbach asked.

Within a year, Auerbach and a nation of fans would learn the answer to that question.

21

The Celtics: Building a Dynasty

In the spring of 1956 Celtic coach Red Auerbach telephoned Ben Kerner, owner of the rival St. Louis Hawks. Red knew that Kerner would be picking ahead of him in the upcoming NBA college draft. Red wanted the NBA rights to Bill Russell, but he was afraid that some other team would draft the tall leaper ahead of him.

"You're picking early," Red told Kerner. "Give me the right to pick in your place, and I'll give you Ed Macauley."

Kerner hesitated. The deal sounded good.

Macauley was a fine shooter, who could be counted on for 20 points a game. Ed wasn't much of a rebounder, but Kerner already had a great rebounder—6-foot-9 Bob Pettit. Kerner knew how badly Auerbach needed a rebounder like Russell, however, so he decided to drive a hard bargain. In addition to Macauley, he demanded Cliff Hagan, a former All-America forward from Kentucky.

Now Red hesitated. He would be giving up two fine players for an inexperienced rookie who might be too skinny to snare the rebounds the Celtics so desperately needed. Although Auerbach had heard many good things about Russell, he'd never actually seen him play. Nevertheless, he eventually agreed: Macauley and Hagan for the rights to Russell.

A few months later Red finally saw Bill play in an exhibition game—much to the coach's dismay. That night a big college center shoved Russell around and made him look like a grade school player. After the game Bill apologized to Auerbach. "I don't usually play that badly," he said.

"I hope you don't," Red said. "If you can't play any better than that, I'll be back coaching in high school."

When the 1956–57 NBA season began, however, Russell was not in the Celtic line-up. He was some 10,000 miles away from Boston—in Melbourne, Australia. There he kept a promise he'd made to President Eisenhower—that he would not turn pro until he had represented the United States in the 1956 Olympics.

Basketball was first played at the Olympics in 1936. The United States won a gold medal that year—and every other year the games were played. Bill's 1956 team was determined to keep up the tradition. They had no trouble at all in the early playoff rounds and easily advanced to the finals.

To win the gold medal, however, the United States would have to defeat a strong team from Russia. The Russians were led by a huge seven-foot center. But next to the

After graduating from the University of San Francisco in 1956, Russell discusses his future with Boston Celtic coach Red Auerbach.

73

bouncy Bill, the Russian giant seemed glued to the floor. Bill and his teammates trounced the Russians, 89–55, to bring home still another gold medal.

Russell came back to America and talked to Red Auerbach about playing for the Celtics. He also met with Abe Saperstein, owner of the Harlem Globetrotters. Abe wanted Bill, the All-American Olympic hero, to draw crowds for his Globetrotters. If the Celtics wanted Russell, they'd have to outbid Saperstein. And after some negotiating, that's just what they did. Bill signed with the Celtics for $25,000 a year, the most ever paid to an NBA rookie—and twice what most NBA veterans were getting.

Auerbach warned Russell that he'd have to work hard for his money. "You must go up there against stronger men and pull those rebounds away from them," Red said. "Then you pass the ball to Cousy. He'll fast-break and get downcourt with three of us against two of them, or two of us against one of them. We've got the scorers, but we need you to get the ball to them."

In Bill's first games he was pushed and shoved away from the hoop by burly centers. But Bill soared higher than the heavier centers to snatch down rebounds and whip the ball to Cousy. In one game Russell seized 16 rebounds.

Bill did more than grab rebounds for the Celtics. His shot-blocking was as awesome in the pros as it had been in college. When an opponent faked a Celtic out of the way and streaked for the hoop, he ran smack into the spread-eagled arms of big Bill. "All by himself," said one NBA coach, "Bill Russell has made the Celtics the best defensive team in the league."

Russell still wasn't shooting much, but that didn't bother Auerbach. "Don't worry about scoring," Red told Bill. "As far as I'm concerned, each of your rebounds is worth two points to a team with our scorers."

Boston's high-scoring Bob Cousy and Bill Sharman each averaged about 20 points a game. And rookie Tommy Heinsohn contributed almost as many. Heinsohn's teammates claimed he took more shots than an anti-aircraft ack-ack gun and laughingly nicknamed him "Ack-Ack." Even the Celtic subs were fine shooters. When the Celtics needed extra fire-power, they could always turn to Frank Ramsey, a former All-America from Kentucky. Coming off the bench in the middle of a close game, Ramsey could score five baskets in a couple of minutes and spur the Celtics to victory. Altogether, the Celtic sharpshooters put in more points—an average of 105 per game—than any other team in the league.

A double threat on offense and defense, the Celtics finished the 1956–57 season first in the NBA East. In the playoff finals they met the St. Louis Hawks. The Hawks had some high scorers of their own, including former Celtics Cliff Hagan and Ed Macauley. But St. Louis's big gun was Bob Pettit, who averaged 25 points a game.

The Celtics and the Hawks battled their way through six games, winning three apiece. The winner of the seventh game would be the new NBA champion. The two teams were neck and neck throughout the crucial game. With a minute left, Boston led, 103–101. Boston Garden was in an uproar. Then Pettit calmly dropped in two free throws to tie up the score. The game went into overtime, and the teams continued their fierce struggle. The overtime was almost a replay of the regular game. With seconds to go the Celtics again took a two-point lead. Then the Hawks let fly a shot that fell in and tied the game once more.

Thousands of fans sat on the edge of their seats as the two tired teams panted into a second overtime. Tension mounted as the lead continued to seesaw back and forth. With two seconds left, the Celtics led, 125–123, and the Hawks called time-out. Their balding player-coach, Alex Hannum, diagrammed a play. When the game resumed, Hannum tossed up a long shot that glanced

In the 1957 Celtics-Hawks playoffs, Bob Cousy (14) feeds the ball to teammate Tommy Heinsohn (above), and Heinsohn takes the shot (below).

off the backboard. Pettit leaped up and tried to tap the rebound into the hoop. The ball hit the front rim, slowly circled the hoop, then fell off just as the final buzzer sounded. The crowd at Boston Garden let out a roar as the exhausted Celtics staggered off the floor with their first NBA championship.

Millions of fans who had watched the game at home on TV fell back into their armchairs, wilted by the tension and excitement of those two overtimes. The names Bob Cousy, Bill Russell, and Bob Pettit had become as well known in American living rooms as the names of baseball's Mickey Mantle and Yogi Berra. And what the Yankees had been to baseball, the Celtics were about to become to basketball—the greatest winning dynasty in the sport.

22

Here Comes Wilt

One March night in 1957 Phog Allen stood on the sideline of a basketball court in Kansas City. Behind him, a huge crowd let out a rising expectant roar as the University of Kansas and University of North Carolina teams trotted onto the floor.

Ever since 1906, when he'd played basketball for Jim Naismith at Kansas, Phog Allen had been a student of the game. He'd seen all the great scorers—Nat Holman, Hank Luisetti, George Mikan—but he'd never seen anyone like Kansas's seven-foot center. "Before he's through," the long-time Kansas coach said, pointing at the huge pivotman, "Wilt Chamberlain will score more points than any man in the history of basketball."

Coaches had been raving about Wilt Chamberlain ever since his school days in Philadelphia. Wilt had led his Overbrook High School team to two state championships, breaking countless scoring records along the way. In his three varsity years, he'd averaged 37 points a game.

Hundreds of college coaches had begged Chamberlain to come play for them. When Wilt chose the University of Kansas, some coaches wondered how coach Allen had lured him out of Philadelphia. For years some coaches had offered small gifts to the best players. But now, according to rumor, the gifts were as large as Cadillac cars.

But all Phog had offered Wilt was tuition, room and board, and books—plus the opportunity to earn $15 a month selling programs at the Kansas football games. "The recruiting of high school players," Allen said, "has become so fierce a struggle that every coach now thinks the other coaches cheat to get the best players."

College coaches had to get the best play-

ers to keep their jobs. Each week the Top Ten teams were ranked in the newspapers. Fans, students, alumni, and even college presidents wanted to see their teams in the Top Ten. Successful teams drew huge

Even in high school, Wilt Chamberlain was head and shoulders above the crowd.

crowds that made money for universities.

In their search for potential All-Americas, coaches scouted high school games all over the country. They also prowled big-city playgrounds, where some of the best players congregated. Most of these youngsters were poor and black, and few of them even dreamed of going to college. They just weren't welcome at most Southern colleges, and they couldn't afford the high tuition costs of most Northern schools. But things began to change in the 1950s. The Civil Rights movement opened doors to blacks. And as more black families became affluent, more black students appeared on college campuses.

Coaches began to offer scholarships to black players. Many of these coaches believed that the best athletes lived in the black ghettos of big cities. "They've played basketball since they were tots," the coaches said, "and they're hungry to get out of the ghetto so they try harder when they play."

Coaches marveled at the skill of these city schoolyard players. They could do stunts that were unknown to white players from the suburbs. Some 5-foot-10 city kids could leap high enough to jam a ball through a hoop with both hands—the slam dunk. They could jump into the air with their backs to the hoop, then flip the ball over their heads and into the hoop—the reverse slam dunk. And they could hover in the air like helicopters to block their rivals' jump shots.

In 1956 the University of Cincinnati found a superb shooter in an Indianapolis slum. His name was Oscar Robertson. A year later, Seattle University discovered a husky forward named Elgin Baylor in a Washington, D.C., ghetto. A fine jump shooter, Baylor was known for his ability to hang in the air while his less agile rivals seemed glued to the ground. "He's never really broken the law of gravity," one admirer observed. "But he's awfully slow about obeying it."

But no black schoolboy was more impressive than the 7-foot-1, 250-pound Wilt Chamberlain. He ran the quarter-mile with an Olympic sprinter's speed. He leaped as high as an Olympic high jumper. He was so strong that the manager of heavyweight boxing champion Floyd Patterson asked Wilt to consider a fight for the heavyweight championship of the world.

Taller than Mikan, as high a leaper as Russell, as agile as Cousy—Wilt was a coach's dream come true. And he certainly knew his way around a basketball court. "When I was growing up," he once said, "I roamed the playgrounds of Philadelphia looking to play against the best players. I learned to do all the things a small man can do with a basketball."

Phog Allen had grinned happily when Wilt agreed to play for the Kansas Jayhawks. But before Wilt's first varsity season (1956–57), the 72-year-old Phog retired and Dick Harp took over as coach. That year Wilt slammed in more than 30 points a game, and Kansas wound up with a 24–2 record. And now, as Phog Allen watched from the sideline, Kansas got set to battle an undefeated University of North Carolina team for the 1957 NCAA championship.

The North Carolina coach, Frank McGuire, had decided on a special game plan to defeat Kansas. He told his 6-foot-5 center, Lennie Rosenbluth, to try to stop Wilt from getting too close to the basket. "Then he can't slam in those dunks," McGuire said. Other coaches had based their whole defense around Wilt, double- and even triple-teaming the Kansas giant. But McGuire told everyone but Rosenbluth to concentrate on the other Jayhawks. "Even if Chamberlain gets thirty points," McGuire reasoned, "we can win by holding down the scoring of the other players."

Wilt bulled past Rosenbluth to score 23 points. But the North Carolina defense held the other Jayhawks in check. It took them three overtimes to do it, but the North

North Carolina's Lenny Rosenbluth puts the pressure on Wilt in the 1957 NCAA finals.

Carolina players finally eked out a 54–53 victory.

Although Kansas lost, Wilt was named the tournament's Most Valuable Player. Yet Wilt knew that many fans had enjoyed seeing him defeated by his much shorter opponent. After the game a bitter Wilt told reporters, "Nobody roots for Goliath," a belief he'd hold throughout his long career.

The following season (1957–58) Wilt continued to dominate the college scene. He, Elgin Baylor, and Oscar Robertson were the only three college players to put in more than 30 points a game. That season the three high scorers made the All-America team along with Guy Rodgers of Temple and Don

Hennon of Pittsburgh (the only white player on the team). It was the first time ever that more than one black man made the team.

That season Wilt led the Jayhawks to an 18–5 record. But when Kansas failed to qualify for the NCAA tournament, most people put the blame on Wilt. "He doesn't win the big games," they said.

Wilt didn't get a chance to prove them wrong because he left Kansas before the next season started. Abe Saperstein offered him $35,000 to join the Globetrotters, and Wilt accepted. "I couldn't afford to say no," he said, explaining that he needed much of the money for his parents back in Philadelphia.

In 1959 the Philadelphia Warriors offered Wilt a salary of $65,000 a season—the most ever paid to an NBA player—and Wilt joined the NBA. As the 1959–60 season dawned, fans waited expectantly for the duel between basketball's two giants—Wilt Chamberlain and Bill Russell.

Wilt soars to the hoop while his Northwestern defenders stand helplessly below.

23
Offense vs. Defense

High-scoring All-Americas such as Wilt Chamberlain and Elgin Baylor made college scoreboards click faster and faster during the 1950s. But in the late '50s and early '60s a number of coaches learned that it took more than points to win a championship.

The 1957–58 season was a forecast of things to come. Ranked number one in the nation was the University of West Virginia. The Mountaineers' high scorer was Jerry West, a willowy 6-foot-3 guard. With Jerry putting in better than 20 points a game, the Mountaineers racked up a 26–2 record.

The second-ranked team that year was the University of Cincinnati. The Bearcats had a sharp-shooting guard of their own—a 6-foot-5 sophomore named Oscar Robertson. Robertson, also known as "The Big O," was the nation's top scorer. In one game at Madison Square Garden he whipped in 56 points—a Garden record. Oscar finished the season with a 35.1 average, and the Bearcats wound up with a 25–3 record.

Most fans expected these two high-scoring teams to collide in the final game of the 1958 NCAA tournament. But strangely enough, neither team got that far. West Virginia was eliminated in the opening round, and Cincinnati didn't make it past the semi-finals.

The finals pitted another high-scoring team, Seattle University, against a strong defensive team, the University of Kentucky. Starring for Seattle was the jump-shooting Elgin Baylor. Baylor was the nation's second-highest scorer, and he was expected to lead Seattle to the championship. But Kentucky coach Adolph Rupp rigged a defense that held down Baylor's scoring, and Kentucky won the crown.

The nation's high scorer in 1957–58, Cincinnati's Oscar Robertson gets off a shot.

The following season Jerry West and Oscar Robertson continued to shoot it out during the regular season. For the second year in a row, Oscar led the nation in scoring, and Jerry wasn't far behind. Both their teams qualified for the 1959 NCAA. But as the two sharpshooters warmed up for the playoffs, a team from the University of California arrived at the tournament with little fanfare. Although California had no high scorers, it had won 22 of 26 games with a sticky defense.

Cincinnati and California met in a semi-final match. The sticky California defense threw up a wall around Oscar, held down his scoring, and defeated the Bearcats, 64–58. Meanwhile, in another semifinal contest, Jerry West and his Mountaineers triumphed over Louisville. The NCAA final was a classic match-up of West Virginia offense versus California defense. The tall California players couldn't contain Jerry West, who drilled in 28 points over their outstretched arms. But they were able to keep the lid on the other Mountaineers and scratch out a 71–70 victory. For the second

OSCAR ROBERTSON ■close-up■

Born on November 24, 1938, Oscar Robertson grew up in a crumbling shack in an Indianapolis slum. When Oscar was six, his older brother nailed a peach basket to the side of the shack. Oscar and his brother Bailey rolled up a ball made of rags and fastened it with some elastic. Tossing that wad of rags at the peach basket, Oscar Robertson sank his first two-pointer.

One day Oscar's mother found an old basketball that had been tossed out by another family and brought it home for her sons. Oscar bounced that ball around the house morning, noon, and night. When the family didn't hear the bam-bam sound of that ball, they knew Oscar was asleep.

By 1955 Oscar was flipping in 20 points a game for Indianapolis's Crispus Attucks High School team. That year Crispus Attucks became the first all-black team to win the Indiana state championship. The following year Oscar arched in 39 points in the tournament finals, and Crispus Attucks won its second straight title.

At the University of Cincinnati Oscar was a three-time All-America. In 1958, 1959, and 1960 he led the nation in scoring, and he finished his career with more points than any college player in basketball history.

After graduation, Oscar was drafted by the NBA Cincinnati Royals. In his rookie year (1960–61) Oscar led the league in assists and was third in the scoring column. Oscar spent most of his pro career in Cincinnati and continued to accumulate points and assists. In 1972 he was traded to the Milwaukee Bucks and helped them win their first NBA championship.

When Oscar retired in 1974, he had a total of 18,000 assists—more than any player in NBA history. He'd scored over 26,000 points, a total exceeded only by Wilt Chamberlain. The Big O got most of those points going one-on-one against his rivals. He'd dribbled closer and closer to the hoop, just daring his defender to stop him.

"If you give him a twelve-foot shot," guard Dick Barnett once said, "Oscar will work on you until he's got a ten-foot shot. Give him ten, he wants eight. Give him eight, he wants six. Give him six, he wants four. Give him four, he wants two. Give him two, you know what he wants? That's right, baby. A lay-up."

straight year, a defense-minded team had bested a high-scoring team for the national championship.

In 1959–60 Cincinnati and West Virginia were again invited to the NCAA tournament. That season Oscar won his third straight national scoring championship. And Jerry averaged 30 points a game, the highest average of his college career. Both players were now seniors. This would be their last chance to win the prize that had eluded them so long—the NCAA crown.

But Jerry and the Mountaineers were eliminated early in the playoffs by a tough team from NYU. And Oscar's Bearcats got only as far as the semi-finals. There they ran into the prickly defense of the California Golden Bears, the team that had stopped them a year earlier. Again the tall Golden Bears batted down shots by Oscar and the other high-scoring Bearcats. California erased Cincinnati, 77–69, and entered the finals in search of its second straight NCAA championship.

The 1960 final was another clear-cut contest between a great defense and a great

JERRY WEST ▪close-up▪

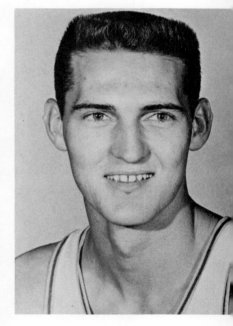

Born on May 28, 1938, Jerry West grew up in a small woodland town in West Virginia. The nearest post office was in Cabin Creek. When Jerry became a pro star, he was known as "Zeke from Cabin Creek" because he never shed the small-town friendliness and amiable drawl of a country boy.

When Jerry was a youngster, a neighbor nailed a hoop to the side of his house. While other boys were off swimming or fishing, Jerry heaved one-handers at the hoop and imagined he was Bob Cousy. "I think I became a basketball player," he once said, "because this is a game a boy can play by himself. . . . I've always been a guy who lives inside himself a lot."

At the age of 11, Jerry was the midget of his grade school team. He was only 5-foot-6 and weighed less than a hundred pounds. But he swished in 12 points a game with his one-handers. "Those one-handed jump shots came naturally to me," he later said. "But I had to work on dribbling and passing and most every aspect of the game. It was a good thing I loved basketball because I had to spend a lot of hours trying to learn it."

During the summer of 1953, Jerry shot up six inches, and by his senior year of high school he stood 6-foot-2. Winging in as many as 45 points in a 32-minute game, he became the highest scorer in the history of West Virginia high school basketball.

After three All-America years at West Virginia, Jerry joined the Los Angeles Lakers in 1960. (The Lakers moved from Minneapolis that year.) In each one of his 13 seasons in the league, he was named to the NBA All-Star team. He played with bandages wrapped around his face. His nose was broken almost a dozen times. "West gets hurt a lot not because he's fragile," a Laker official said. "He gets hurt because he goes all out and takes chances that others don't take."

By the time Jerry retired in 1974, he had scored more than 25,000 points, topping everyone but Wilt Chamberlain and Oscar Robertson. And no player scored more points than West in playoff games. In 153 pressure-packed playoff games, Jerry calmly tossed in an average of 29 points per game.

"I sometimes feel that everything I toss up will go in," Jerry once said. And sometimes that didn't seem to be much of an exaggeration!

81

Some Holy Cross defenders take extreme measures to keep West Virginia's high-scoring Jerry West from doing his thing.

offense. During the regular season California had given up fewer points than any team in the nation (50 per game). And its opponent, Ohio State, had scored more points than any team in the nation (90 per game). The Ohio State center was 6-foot-8 Jerry Lucas, the most accurate shooter in the nation. Lucas was surrounded by four other excellent shooters—John Havlicek, Mel Nowell, Larry Siegfried, and Joe Roberts. All five Ohio State starters would later become pros.

In this match-up the Ohio State offense washed over the California defense like a tidal wave. The Buckeyes won, 75–55, and were crowned the 1960 NCAA champions. Although a good offense had finally triumphed, many coaches were impressed by how often in the past few years strong defensive teams had come out on top.

Ed Jucker, a new coach at the University of Cincinnati, decided to make some changes in the Bearcats' game plan. "You don't have to teach today's kids how to shoot," Jucker said. "They do it naturally. So you have plenty of time to teach them how to play defense."

Before the 1960–61 season began, the Big O graduated and joined the pros. But the Bearcats didn't seem to miss him much. Playing a tight defense, they won 26 of 29 games and climbed all the way to the NCAA finals. There they met the defending NCAA champions from Ohio State. Led by Jerry Lucas and John Havlicek, the Buckeyes hadn't lost a game all year.

More than 17,000 fans crammed into a Kansas City arena to watch the Ohio State offense and the Cincinnati defense battle it out for the NCAA championship. And this time the defense won, as Cincinnati upset Ohio State, 70–65. The Buckeyes cried "fluke" and swore they'd get revenge.

The Buckeyes got a rematch—but no revenge—in the 1962 NCAA finals. Again Ohio State was pitted against Cincinnati, and again the Cincinnati defense held up.

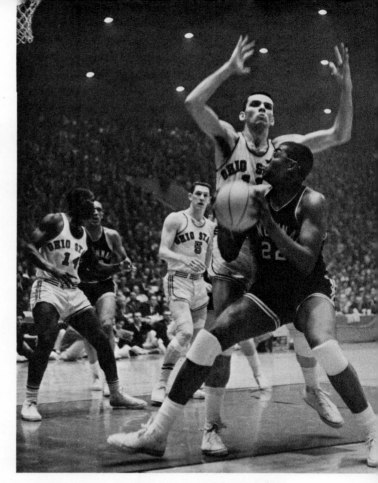

Paul Hogue gets set to shoot despite the intimidating presence of Ohio State's Jerry Lucas. In the background is John Havlicek (5).

With a decisive 71–59 victory, the Bearcats won their second straight NCAA title.

The following year the Bearcats tried to make it three in a row. By then Cincinnati was regarded as the best defensive team in the nation. "We keep hoping that one day we'll shut someone out," said one of the Bearcats, only half-jokingly.

Cincinnati needed all that defense in the '63 NCAA finals. There they met the Loyola Ramblers, the highest-scoring team in the nation. The two teams were so evenly matched that the game went into overtime, but Loyola eventually squeaked through to a 60–58 victory.

Despite Cincinnati's defeat, more and more coaches were now convinced that a team needed more than high scorers to win a championship. A gluey defense had lifted the University of Cincinnati Bearcats to within one basket of becoming the first team ever to win three straight NCAA titles.

24

The Celtics: Rolling On

The referee tossed the ball high into the air. Bill Russell of the Boston Celtics and Wilt Chamberlain of the Philadelphia Warriors leaped up for the tap. Some 14,000 fans peered down at the action on the brightly lit court at Boston Garden. And all across the country, millions more sat in front of their TV sets to watch this long-awaited duel of giants.

On this November afternoon in 1959 almost every fan had two questions on his mind: Could the great defensive player Russell stop the great offensive player Chamberlain? And could Chamberlain and his Warriors stop Bill and the Celtics from winning their third NBA championship in four years?

The Celtics had won their first championship in 1956–57, Russell's rookie season. Bill had played a major role in that victory, grabbing the rebounds that fed the Boston scoring machine. The following year Bill and the Celtics had seemed a sure bet to repeat their triumph. But Bill sprained his

Wilt Chamberlain shoots over Bill Russell in the first of many duels between the two big centers.

ankle in the playoff finals. While he watched from the sidelines, the St. Louis Hawks walked off with the championship. Then, with a healthy Russell back in the line-up, the Celtics came back in 1958–59 to win their second NBA crown.

As the 1959–60 season got under way, however, many people thought that Bill and his Celtics would finally meet their match. A new supercenter had just entered the league—7-foot-1 Wilt Chamberlain. In his first few NBA games the highly heralded rookie had more than lived up to his billing. But now he was facing the best center in the league. And Russell was looking to cut him down to size.

But stopping Wilt was easier said than done, as Russell soon found out. Early in the game the ball hopped off the hoop, and the two big men leaped for the rebound. Right away Russell felt Wilt's awesome strength. "I started to take the ball away from Chamberlain," Bill later recalled. "Did you ever try to bend a lamp post with your bare hands? That's how rigid Wilt's arms were. Then he began to pull on me. I actually felt my feet leaving the floor. I'm going to look awfully silly, I thought, if he stuffs the ball and me through the basket. Fortunately, the ref blew the whistle for a held ball."

Bill refused to be intimidated by the huge Warrior. The next time a Philadelphia shot missed the hoop, it was Russell who came down with the rebound. He lined the ball to Bob Cousy, and the slender Celtic guard put in a two-pointer. For the rest of the game Russell was the dominant figure at both ends of the court. On offense, he fed the ball to Cousy, Bill Sharman, Frank Ramsey, and Tommy Heinsohn. And on defense, he blocked one shot after another, making Chamberlain fight for every point he got.

Wilt struggled to keep the Warriors in the game, but it was a losing battle. The Celtics won, 115–106. In this first duel between the giants, Russell had scored 22 points and limited Chamberlain to 30 (below Wilt's usual total). And Russell had snared 38 rebounds to Wilt's 35.

That first confrontation set a pattern that held up throughout the season. In the games that followed, Russell usually limited Chamberlain to 30 points or less, and the Celtics usually won. But then the Celtics almost always won—no matter whom they played. In one stretch, Bill and the Celtics defeated just about every team in the league, winning 17 games in a row.

But Boston wasn't a one-man team. In fact, many fans thought that Cousy deserved the lion's share of credit for the Celtics' success. Although Cousy was now 32 years old, he certainly hadn't slowed down much.

"Bob Cousy scores twenty points a game for us," said one of his biggest fans, coach Red Auerbach. "And in the average game he gets ten assists. Those ten assists mean twenty more points. So he accounts for forty points a game. What Bill Russell does for us on defense, Bob Cousy does on offense."

Led by Cousy and Russell, the Celtics finished the 1959–60 season first in the NBA East. They erased Philadelphia in the playoffs, then took on the St. Louis Hawks in the finals.

The teams split the first six games, each winning three. As the seventh match began, the 1960 NBA championship was still up for grabs. In the early minutes of the game the veteran Cousy looked exhausted. But before long, the Hawks were the ones who needed a rest. Leading the Celtic fast-break, Cousy ran them ragged. Bob scored 19 points and collected 14 assists to lead Boston to a 112–103 victory. In this winner-take-all seventh game, the Celtics had picked up their second NBA title in a row, their third in four years.

In the 1960–61 season the champions faced an array of high-scoring challengers. The league leader was Chamberlain, who popped in 38 points per game, more than any player in NBA history. The Lakers (now based in Los Angeles) had the NBA's number two scorer—Elgin Baylor, the former Seattle All-America. In one game Baylor collected a record-breaking 71 points. The Celtics also had to contend with Oscar Robertson, now a rookie with the Cincinnati Royals. In his first pro year the Big O was averaging a big 30 points a game.

But the Boston defense held firm. Again the Celtics finished first in the East, and again they faced the Hawks in the finals. This time the Celtics raced past the Hawks in five games to capture their third NBA title in a row.

The following season (1961–62) Wilt again led the league in scoring. In one game against New York he poured in a record-shattering 100 points. And he averaged 50 points a game over the season, another record. It seemed that no one could stop Wilt— no one but the Celtics, that is. Despite Wilt's incredible offense, the Celtics consistently beat the Warriors.

In the playoffs the Celtics eliminated the Warriors in the semi-finals, then faced the Los Angeles Lakers in the finals. Los Angeles was a young team with a great deal of fire-power. In addition to Elgin Baylor,

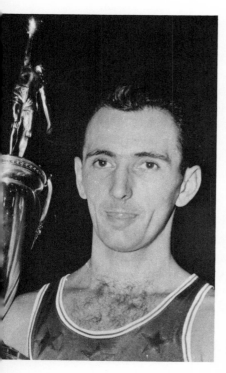

BOB COUSY ▪ close-up ▪

Bob Cousy dribbled toward the right side of the court. Suddenly he bounced the ball behind his back and cut toward the left side of the hoop. His opponent stared, flatfooted and flabbergasted, as Cousy tossed in a lay-up.

Moments later Cousy drove down the middle of the court. As Bob soared toward the basket, the rival defenseman rose to block his shot. Still in midair, Bob whirled the ball behind his back and fed it to a teammate on his right. The teammate, all alone, curled in the lay-up.

Those magical behind-the-back dribbles and passes earned Bob a nickname—the Houdini of Hardwood. A 6-foot-1 New Yorker with a juggler's quick hands, Cousy learned those tricks at Holy Cross in Worcester, Massachusetts. An All-America guard, Cousy was one of the best college players in the country. The idol of fans all over New England, he was especially popular in Boston.

When Cousy graduated in 1950, local fans assumed that he would be the Boston Celtics' number one draft choice. But Celtic coach Red Auerbach had other ideas. Auerbach didn't want any 6-foot-1 backcourt wizards. He wanted a 6-foot-11 center. "You win with the big guys," Red explained.

Bob ended up with the NBA Chicago Stags. But the Stags went out of business before he had played a single game. When the Stags folded, their players were made available to other teams. Boston, the New York Knicks, and the Philadelphia Warriors clamored for the two Chicago stars—Max Zaslofsky and Andy Phillip—but no one wanted Cousy. To settle the squabble, NBA commissioner Maurice Podoloff put the names of Zaslofsky, Phillip, and Cousy into a hat. The Knicks reached into the hat and pulled out Zaslofsky's name. The Warriors reached in and picked Phillip. Both teams were overjoyed. The disappointed Celtics had to settle for Cousy.

Before long, however, Red Auerbach's disappointment turned to delight. Almost every season Bob led the Celtics in scoring and assists. Best of all, he was a real "clutch" player. Cousy's greatest performances came in the pressure-packed playoff games.

In a 1953 playoff against Syracuse, the Celtics were behind by a point with the Laker offense featured Jerry West, the former West Virginia star. Although this was only Jerry's second year in the NBA, he was already one of the best shooters in the league.

The young Lakers battled the Celtic veterans to another winner-take-all seventh game. That game, too, went down to the wire. As the final seconds of the final championship game ticked away, the teams were deadlocked, 100–all.

The Lakers' Frank Selvy had the ball—and time for just one shot. Selvy had once scored 100 points in a college game, but now he was going for the most important two-pointer of his career. If he made this basket, the Lakers would be the new NBA champs, and the Celtic reign would end. Selvy tossed up a short jumper just before the clock ran out. The ball hit the rim, hopped across the open basket, struck the far rim—and bounced away. The game went into overtime, and Boston rallied to win its fourth straight championship title.

The Celtics began the 1962–63 season aiming for number five. By now Boston had added some younger players to its roster. Playing both guard and forward was a rookie

only one second left. Cousy had the ball. He'd already scored 24 points in the game, but all his efforts would be wasted if he couldn't score now. As Bob lunged toward the hoop, a desperate Syracuse defender fouled him. Bob went to the free-throw line. Cousy knew that the whole game hung on this one shot, but that didn't rattle him. He calmly tossed in a free throw to tie the game.

In overtime the Celtics again trailed by a point with one second left. Again Bob was fouled, and again he kept the Celtics alive by making his free throw.

In the second overtime Syracuse led, 90–88, with only a few seconds left. When Cousy got the ball, the crowd began to cheer. With time running out again, Bob flung up a running one-hander that swooped through the nets and sent the game into still another overtime.

With three seconds remaining in the third overtime, the Celtics were once more behind by a basket. This time Bob connected with a one-hander from 25 feet out and plunged the game into a fourth overtime. By now the fans at Boston Garden were in a frenzy.

The crowd kept on roaring throughout that fourth overtime. Syracuse leaped out to a five-point lead, but then Bob ripped nine points through the hoop. The Celtics won, 111–105. Bob had scored 50 points—almost half the Boston total. And 25 of them had been in overtime, when one miss could have meant defeat.

In his later years with the Celtics, Bob gave up scoring a lot of points to concentrate on feeding the ring of Celtic shooters. As the Celtic captain, he led his team to five straight NBA championships.

After that fifth championship, "The Cooz," as teammates called him, retired and became a coach. He left the NBA as its fourth-highest scorer and its all-time leader in assists. In 1962 a hundred sports editors named him the NBA's all-time greatest player. Other players would pass him on the scoring list, and his record for assists would also be smashed. But to this day, when a coach sees a really slick guard and wants to give him the highest praise, the coach is likely to say, "He's another Cooz."

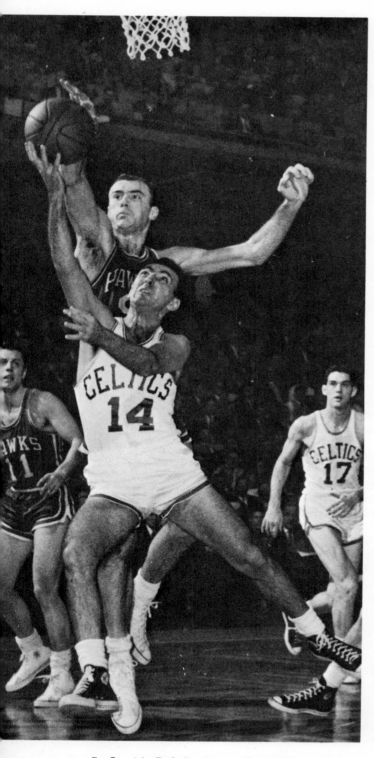

St. Louis's Bob Pettit gets his hand on the ball as Bob Cousy (14) tries to flip it in the hoop.

from Ohio State—John Havlicek. Coming off the bench to give Cousy and Sharman a rest were guards K.C. Jones and Sam Jones (no relation). And filling in for Tommy Heinsohn was Satch Sanders.

As usual, the Celtics rolled home first in the East. In the playoffs they squeezed past Oscar Robertson and the Cincinnati Royals in seven games. ("Do the Celtics ever lose a seventh game?" a frustrated Royal asked.)

Once again the Celtics faced the Lakers in the NBA finals. The Celtics were especially eager to win this championship. Only two other pro teams had ever won five championships in a row—baseball's Yankees and hockey's Canadiens. More important, Bob Cousy would be retiring at the end of the season. He wanted to go out a winner, and his teammates were determined to see that he did.

After winning three of the first five games, the charged-up Celtics took an early lead in the sixth game. A win here would mean the championship. But in the fourth quarter, with Boston ahead by nine points, a tired Cousy sprained his ankle and limped off to the locker room. Without their captain, the Celtics seemed to fall apart. The Lakers closed to within one point. Cousy dragged himself back from the dressing room and onto the court. Although he couldn't do much in the way of shooting, he got his teammates moving again. He fed the ball to Heinsohn, then to Russell, and then to Sharman.

On track again, Boston held onto its lead. With seconds to go, the Celtics were ahead, 112–109. And to make sure they stayed there, Cousy dribbled out the clock. At the buzzer that ended the game and his Celtic career, a jubilant Cousy threw the ball high into the air. His Celtics had done what no other basketball team had ever done—won five straight championships.

But now Cousy was leaving the Celtics. Could they go on winning without him?

During the 1963 NBA finals Boston's Bill Russell and Los Angeles's Elgin Baylor battle for a rebound *(above)*, and Cousy makes one of his famous behind-the-back passes *(below)*.

25

UCLA: Another Dynasty

*With every starter coming back
Yes, Walt and Gail and Keith and Jack,
And Fred and Freddie and some more
We could be champs in sixty-four.*

UCLA coach John Wooden scribbled down those lines of verse as he rode in an airliner one evening in the spring of 1963. He and his Bruins were on their way home from a road trip. And although the team had just lost two straight games, Wooden was envisioning an NCAA championship for UCLA in the 1963–64 season.

The former "India Rubber Man" had come to the University of California at Los Angeles in 1948. In those days, UCLA was anything but a basketball power. Most Southern California boys liked such outdoor sports as swimming, surfing, and tennis. They weren't at all inclined to spend their time shooting fouls in a stuffy gym. But Wooden was determined to mold a strong team. He drilled his players for hours at a time and kept them running throughout the long practice sessions.

"Nine out of every ten games are won or lost in the last five minutes," he told them. "The team that's in better shape is going to win those close games."

Wooden's first UCLA team had been expected to finish last in its conference in the 1948–49 season. To everyone's surprise but Wooden's they led the conference's Southern Division with a 22–7 record. And in the years that followed, the Bruins developed into a truly competitive team. But try as they might, the Bruins always fell short of a national championship.

When it came to scoring points, the Bruins had no problems. Wooden had taught them

UCLA coach John Wooden, the old "India Rubber Man" from Purdue.

the lickety-split fast-break offense he'd learned at Purdue in the 1930s. But if the Bruins were to win a championship, they'd have to improve their defense.

In the early 1960s Wooden began to teach a defense that was as hectic as his offense. As soon as the opposing team passed the ball inbounds, the UCLA defense would go into action. Two or more Bruins would scurry around the man with the ball and try to wall him in. Hopefully, the ballhandler would get so flustered that he'd lose his dribble or make a desperate pass that could be intercepted. Wooden called this harrying defense the UCLA full-court press. Before long, rival coaches would call it the Monster.

At the start of the 1963–64 season Wooden believed he had the makings of a real championship team—five players with the speed to fast-break on offense and press all over the court on defense. "I've never had a team with such quickness," he said. "They're like mice out there."

The only trouble was, Wooden's players were mouselike in size as well as speed. UCLA's tallest player was the 6-foot-5 Fred Slaughter, who had to crane his neck to look up at opposing centers. At guard were the 6-foot-1 Gail Goodrich, also known as "Stumpy," and 6-foot-2 Walt Hazzard. The forwards were 6-foot-5 Keith Erickson and 6-foot-3 Jack Hirsch.

Nevertheless, the Bruins were more than a match for their tallest rivals. "What they lacked in height," wrote one reporter, "they made up in long arms, quick hands, and lightning feet."

Early that season, UCLA met a much taller team from Washington State. The Bruins were trailing, 15–14, when Wooden signaled for his full-court press. Two Bruins trapped a Washington State ballhandler, who tried to fling the ball crosscourt to a teammate. But Goodrich intercepted the pass and scored a two-pointer. A little later the UCLA defense caused another turnover. This time Hazzard stole the ball and cruised in for a lay-up. The Washington players were helpless against the Monster, and the Bruins romped to a 121–77 victory.

Although the Bruins got off to a good start in 1963–64, few UCLA students were aware of their progress. The team practiced in a smelly gym called "Body Odor Barn" by the players. UCLA had no huge campus field house, and the Bruins played their home games in two different arenas—one of which was 25 miles from the campus.

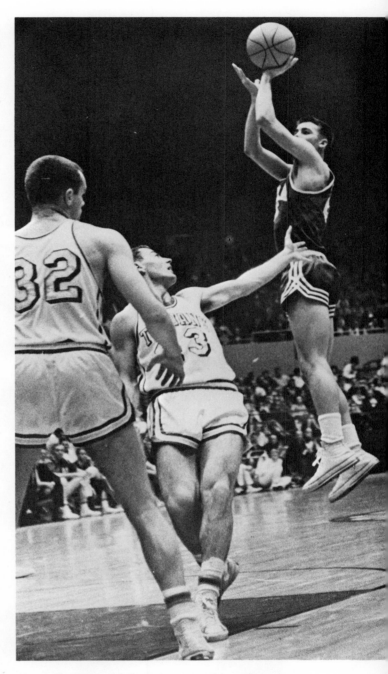

Little Gail Goodrich shoots over his taller opponents in a 1964 game.

Only the most avid fans were willing to travel that distance to watch a game.

But as the season progressed, fans began flocking to those arenas. UCLA picked up one victory after another. In fact, the Bruins didn't lose one game all year. Ranked number one in the nation, they entered the NCAA tournament. UCLA scrambled past Seattle and San Francisco before facing Duke University in the finals.

Two of the Duke players stood 6-foot-10, and nearly all of them towered over the Bruins. To win the championship, the UCLA "mice" would really have to run. Before the game began the Bruins assembled in the dressing room. They were expecting a big pep talk from their coach, but Wooden had just one thing to say. "Who can remember which team finished second in the NCAA two years ago?" he asked.

Not surprisingly, no one recalled that the also-ran team was Ohio State. "That one question," Gail Goodrich said later, "was all the coach really had to say—and he knew it."

Going up for a basket, UCLA's Kenny Washington is fouled by Jeff Mullins of Duke.

As soon as the game began, the Bruins were off and running. On defense, they snatched passes, stole dribbles, and totally demoralized the Duke Blue Devils. On offense, they sped past the slower Duke players for uncontested lay-ups. Goodrich flipped in 27 points, pacing the Bruins to a 98–83 victory—and their first NCAA championship.

Before the start of the 1964–65 season, Jack Hirsch, Fred Slaughter, and Walt Hazzard all graduated. The 6-foot-2 Kenny Washington joined Goodrich in the backcourt; 6-foot-6 Edgar Lacey teamed up with Keith Erickson at forward; and 6-foot-7 Mike Lynn took over at center. Although three of Wooden's five champion starters were missing, the coach was optimistic about the newcomers. "I've got a little more height this season," Wooden told reporters. "And I hope I have the same amount of speed."

In their first game of the season, the Bruins faced Illinois. UCLA went into that contest with a 30-game winning streak from the previous season. But the Illini promptly cut the string. Weaving through a surprisingly spotty Bruin defense, Illinois picked up an easy 110–83 victory.

The Bruin players were stunned by their poor showing, but Wooden took the defeat in stride. "The pressure of the winning streak is off now," he said encouragingly. "Now just go out and play your game."

For the rest of the season the Bruins did just that. Their defense solidified, and the Monster press was as intimidating as ever. The offense improved, too, and Goodrich upped his average to 25 points. The Bruins finished the season with an excellent 24–2 record and were ranked number two in the nation behind Michigan.

The two top teams met in the 1965 NCAA final. Michigan's star was 6-foot-5 Cazzie Russell, a high-scoring jump shooter. Cazzie and Gail Goodrich had made the 1965 All-America team along with Miami's

Michigan's Cazzie Russell dribbles past Washington in the 1965 NCAA finals.

Rick Barry, Princeton's Bill Bradley, and Davidson's Fred Hetzel.

A huge crowd turned out to see the two All-Americas battle for the championship. Michigan leaped out ahead as Russell tossed in eight quick points. But UCLA fought back with the Monster. Dazzled by wind-milling arms, the Michigan players made one turnover after another. They threw the ball away, kicked it away, and bobbled it away. The Bruins scooped up the loose balls and ran for lay-ups.

Then the Bruin offense took over. Good-rich slammed in 42 points, the most ever in an NCAA final. By a score of 91–80 UCLA became the fifth team in NCAA history to win two titles in a row.

That summer a gleaming new building began to rise on the UCLA campus. It was Pauley Pavilion, the new home court of the Bruins. Some 13,000 fans would be able to watch games from its comfortable seats. It was a far cry from "Body Odor Barn." But within a year the new building would barely accommodate the thousands of fans who would come to see Johnny Wooden's newest and greatest star.

For while Pauley Pavilion was rising, a slender 7-foot-1 young man rose at a press conference in New York City. He was the most sought-after high school player in the history of basketball. He announced that he had decided to attend UCLA. The young man's name was Lewis Ferdinand Alcindor. The second stage of a dynasty was about to begin.

26

The Celtics: After Cousy

Before the 1963–64 season began, a steady stream of reporters came to interview Bill Russell. And almost every one asked the same question: Could the Celtics win a sixth straight championship without their retired quarterback, Bob Cousy?

Time and again, Russell gave the same answer: "Yes." And then he'd add, "Cousy was great, but we were never a one-man team."

The Celtics were missing more than Cousy, however. His backcourt partner, Bill Sharman, had also retired. Replacing the two veteran guards were the Jones boys. K.C. was a tenacious defender, Sam a bulls-eye shooter. The forwards were Tommy Heinsohn, now 30, but still the same old "Ack-Ack" shooter, and Tom "Satch" Sanders, a dependable scorer and an abso-lute leech on defense. The swingman, alter-nating between the guard and forward spots, was sophomore John Havlicek. As a rookie John had had some trouble with his shoot-ing. But during the summer of 1963 he'd thrown hundreds of jumpers in a steamy gym in Ohio as he sweated to become a really good shooter.

Of course, the Celtic center was still big Bill Russell. The 29-year-old pivotman was now a fine all-around player. He had de-veloped into a steady scorer, chipping in about 16 points a game. And his defense was better than ever. Shooting, rebounding, and blocking shots—Russell did it all. But as the new season got under way, Red Auer-bach asked Russell to take on another chore. He wanted Russell to be the "safetyman" in Auerbach's version of the full-court defense that John Wooden was teaching his UCLA players 3,000 miles away.

Like Wooden, Auerbach had noticed that many of the modern ballplayers were not good ballhandlers. "They take so many jump shots," Auerbach said, "that they don't bother to practice their dribbling." To take advantage of that weakness, Auerbach told

John Havlicek (17) puts in a two-pointer for the Celtics in a game against the Knicks.

his Celtics to swarm all over a weak ball-handler and try to make him cough up the ball. "Leave your man and play the ball," he told the Celtics.

But the full-court press was dangerous. The danger, of course, was that if the Celtics doubled up on the ballhandler, they'd be leaving one or more of his teammates unguarded. If the ballhandler didn't panic, he might get the ball to an open man, who could drop in an uncontested shot. As safety-man, it would be Russell's job to see that that didn't happen. If a rival did get free,

Bill would be stationed under the hoop to block his shot.

Russell did all that was asked of him, and the Celtics got off to a fast start in 1963–64. With their pressing defense and fast-breaking offense, they hardly missed Cousy and Sharman. John Havlicek led the team in scoring with 20 points a game. His summer of practice had paid off.

The Celtics streaked to first place in the East. In the playoffs they defeated the Cincinnati Royals to reach the finals against the San Francisco Warriors. There they faced

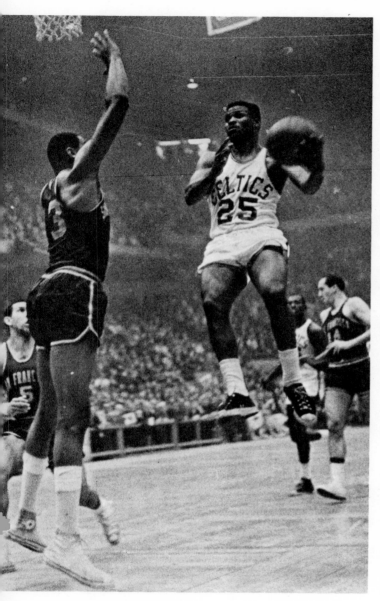

K.C. Jones leaps high off the ground in an attempt to shoot over Wilt Chamberlain.

1964 NBA finals, the Warrior defense was powerless against the Celtic fast-break. And the Celtics' ball-stealing defense put a lid on the Warrior offense. The Celtics defeated the Warriors in five games to become the first pro team ever to win six straight championships.

The Celtics continued to dominate the league in 1964–65. That year they totaled 62 victories, an NBA record. With an exciting defense and fast-paced offense, the Celtics drew crowds whenever they played. They helped boost NBA attendance to an all-time high of almost three million.

Millions more watched them on TV during the 1965 playoffs. And in the semifinals those fans saw one of the most exciting NBA playoff games ever. It was another seventh, winner-take-all battle for the Celtics, this time against the Philadelphia 76ers. Playing now for the 76ers was Wilt Chamberlain, who had been traded by San Francisco. In the closing seconds of this seventh game, the Celtics were ahead, 110–109, but their dynasty hung by a single point. Hal Greer of the 76ers had the ball—out of bounds, only a few feet from the basket. If the 76ers could put the ball into the hoop, the mighty Celtics would be dethroned.

As he gripped the ball out of bounds, Greer looked for the upstretched hands of Chamberlain. But Russell was leaning on Chamberlain, cutting him off from the pass. As Greer tossed the ball toward another Warrior, John Havlicek dashed away from his own man—playing the ball, as Auerbach had taught. The crowd roared as Havlicek got a hand on the ball and deflected it toward a Celtic. The buzzer ripped through the bedlam. The game ended with the Celtics still ahead, 110–109.

The championship finals were almost anticlimactic. The Celtics swept by the Lakers in five games to win their seventh straight NBA crown—their eighth in nine years. Not since 1958 had any team but the Celtics won the NBA championship.

a familiar foe—Wilt Chamberlain. Wilt and the Warriors had changed their home base from Philadelphia to San Francisco. The Syracuse Nats had replaced them in Philadelphia and were now called the Philadelphia 76ers.

During the regular season, the Warrior defense had given up only 102 points per game, the fewest in the league. But in the

If any team was going to topple the Celtic dynasty, the 1965–66 season seemed the perfect time to do it. By then Tommy Heinsohn had retired. The 32-year-old Russell was slowing down. Even K.C. and Sam Jones were over 30, and both needed frequent breathers.

The Philadelphia 76ers, meanwhile, looked stronger than ever. In addition to Wilt, the 76ers had a squad of jump-shooting marksmen—Greer, Billy Cunningham, and Chet Walker. And anything they missed was invariably tapped in by the 6-foot-10 Luke Jackson. The high-scoring 76ers came from behind late in the season to catch the Celtics and finish first in the NBA East.

The 1966 playoffs began. In the opening round the Celtics met the Cincinnati Royals and their sharpshooting duo of Jerry Lucas and Oscar Robertson. The Royals jumped out to lead, two games to one, in the best-of-five series. The Royals had the home-court advantage for game four, and they needed only this one win to eliminate the Celtics. But Boston was always at its best under pressure, and this was no exception. The Celtics evened up the series with a resounding 120–103 victory, then won the next game to advance to the semi-finals.

Next they opposed the 76ers' Wilt and his flock of high scorers. But the old Celtics seemed rejuvenated by their come-from-behind victory over the Royals. Russell soared like a fresh-faced rookie, snatching rebounds and slamming down shots, as the Celtics swept by the 76ers in five games and entered their tenth NBA final in ten years.

Again they took on the Los Angeles Lakers, who had been defeated by the Celtics in four of those finals. But this seemed to be the Lakers' year. In the first game, on the Boston home court, Jerry West and Elgin Baylor sparked Los Angeles to a 133–129 victory over the Celtics.

That night Red Auerbach announced that after the playoffs ended he would leave his coaching job to become the team's front-

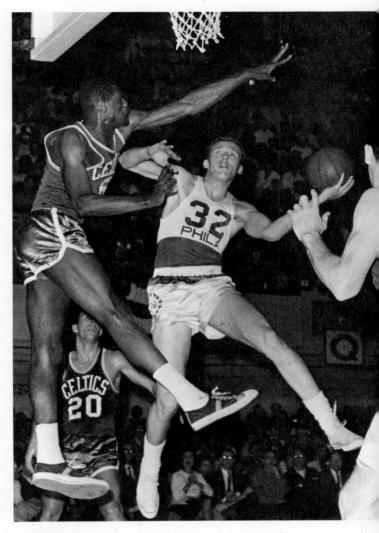

Philadelphia's Billy Cunningham is stopped by the long arm of Bill Russell.

office general manager. The new Celtic coach, announced a smiling Red, would be Bill Russell.

The appointment of a black coach made front-page headlines in newspapers all over the country. "It's about time," many people said. Two of every three players in the NBA were black, and almost half the players in pro baseball and football were black. Yet Russell would be the first black man to coach a big-league pro team.

The news seemed to electrify the Celtics. They blew by the Lakers in the next three

Surrounded by Celtics, Laker Jerry West goes straight to the basket in the 1966 playoffs.

games to lead the finals, three games to one. But then the Lakers retaliated with back-to-back wins and tied the series at three games all. Once again the Celtics dragged themselves into a do-or-die seventh game, their fourth since 1962.

The two teams fought a fierce defensive battle. Near the end of the game the Celtics surged ahead to lead, 95–87. With only 15 seconds left, the desperate Lakers struck back with six quick points, closing the gap to 95–93. But then the clock ran out, and the Celtics had their eighth straight championship. Red Auerbach puffed a victory cigar as he and his players trotted off the Boston Garden court to the cheers of their fans.

The Celtics had given their all to win that championship. But how much longer, new coach Bill Russell had to wonder, could he and these aging Celtics stretch out their dynasty?

27

Changing Times

As the 1966–67 season began, the National Basketball Association could look back to 1946 when it began as the Basketball Association of America. The NBA had come a long way in those 20 years and was now as big league as baseball or football.

The NBA was truly a national league. It now had ten teams stretched across the land from New York to California. Attendance had soared from the one-million mark in the fifties to more than three million.

NBA stars earned as much money as baseball's Mickey Mantle and football's Jim Brown. Both Wilt Chamberlain and Bill Russell made more than $100,000 a season. And a Knick rookie, Cazzie Russell, had been given a three-year contract for $250,-000.

The influx of black players had changed the game itself. The blacks had brought their fierce one-on-one duels from the ghetto playgrounds. When a pro player slammed the ball through the hoop with two hands, that slam dunk was his way of telling an opponent, "I am the boss!" When his opponent replied a minute later with a slam dunk—or, even more emphatically, with a *reverse* slam dunk—fans sat on the edge of their seats, waiting for the next move.

The black players—and white players such as Rick Barry, who copied their style—made the game a lot faster than the game of the 1950s. Next to these soaring players, most of the 1950s stars would have looked like plodders. In 1953 a team of George Mikan, Bob Cousy, Bob Davies, Paul Arizin, and Dolph Schayes would have been considered the all-time "dream team." But each of those players would have had a hard time making the 1966 NBA All-Star team of

Rick Barry, Jerry Lucas, Wilt Chamberlain, Oscar Robertson, and Jerry West—a team that not even Bill Russell could make! That year Bill was on the All-Star second team.

But in 1966 the biggest change of all seemed to be just around the corner. For the first time since the late 1950s the Celtics weren't the odds-on favorite to win the NBA title. Many fans and experts were predicting that the Philadelphia 76ers would be the new champs.

The 76ers still had all their old sharpshooters—Billy Cunningham, Hal Greer, Chet Walker, and Luke Jackson. And, most important, the 76ers had what they called "a new Wilt Chamberlain." Before the 1966–67 season began, Philadelphia coach Alex Hannum had had a long talk with Wilt. Hannum realized that it would take more than a great offense to win a championship. And Hannum thought that Wilt could provide that something more.

"You have Luke Jackson to pull down rebounds and tap in points around our basket," Hannum told Wilt. "And you are surrounded by excellent shooters. You don't have to score fifty points for us to win. If you get twenty, the other guys will get the rest. Instead of working hard on offense, I want you to work harder at the other end of the court. I want you to pull down rebounds to start our fast-break. And I want you to block shots that will subtract eight, ten, or twelve points from the other team."

That was fine with Wilt. No one wanted the championship more than he did. "I'd give up *all* my points to be on a championship team," Chamberlain said.

In the 1966–67 season, Wilt did everything Hannum asked—and more. The results

Wilt gets set to dunk the ball—with no interference from his defenders.

were dramatic. Chamberlain concentrated on defense and pulled down more rebounds than anyone in the league. Although his scoring dropped to 24 points, that didn't hurt the 76ers. His teammates picked up the slack, and Philadelphia averaged 125 points a game to lead the NBA on offense. Best of all, they finished the season in first place

WILT CHAMBERLAIN ▪close-up▪

Wilt Chamberlain's great height gave him an obvious advantage on a basketball court. But Wilt considered his size a mixed blessing. "I know that some people consider me a freak," he once said. "I've had to learn to live with that, and it isn't easy."

From the time Chamberlain was a 6-foot-11 Philadelphia high school boy, he was known as "Wilt the Stilt." He glared when he heard the name. He much preferred to be called "the Dipper," a name he was given because of the graceful way he dipped a ball into a basket with his fallaway one-handers.

All during his pro career Chamberlain insisted he stood only 7-foot-1. But 6-foot-10 centers had to tilt their heads to look up at him. Some newspapermen once measured the height of a doorway. The doorway was seven feet and three inches high. Yet Wilt had to duck his head when he stepped through that doorway.

Wilt became the highest scorer in the history of the NBA. Yet, strangely enough, he was one of the league's worst free-throw shooters. Most seasons he put in only five of every ten of his shots from the foul line. Coaches said he took the shot too quickly. Friends said he wanted to rush off the line because he felt embarrassed as he stood there alone and exposed.

Wilt certainly wanted to be as inconspicuous as possible. "My ambition is to walk down a street and have no one pay any attention to me unless I spoke to them," he once told a friend. "It's rough when you can't get away from being a celebrity. Movie stars can put on dark glasses and no one knows who they are. What good are dark glasses for a man who's seven foot tall?"

But Wilt stood out in any crowd, especially when he was playing basketball. And it wasn't just his great height that made people stare—it was also his great talent.

In his first NBA season (1959–60) the super-rookie had an incredible average of 37 points a game. In one game he actually put in 100 points, an NBA record that still stands today. And during the 1966–67 season he connected with more than seven of every ten shots he took from the floor— another league standard.

Altogether Wilt put in more than 31,000 points during his 14 NBA seasons. He also pulled down a total of 23,924 rebounds, more than any other player. Wilt was practically a one-man basketball team, yet many people considered him a loser. His critics charged that Wilt folded in the big games. When his teams failed to win a championship, the blame always fell on Chamberlain.

Wilt shrugged off the critics, however. "If I dropped onto a basketball court from another planet tomorrow," he once said, "no one would be talking about anyone except me. They'd still consider me the greatest."

Was he the greatest? He certainly didn't win as many championships as Bill Russell. He wasn't as versatile as Oscar Robertson. But just about the most important thing a basketball player can do is take the ball and put it into the basket. And no one did that more often than Wilt Chamberlain.

with a record-breaking 68–13 mark.

But the 76ers weren't champions yet—many people were betting they never would be. The 76ers might meet the Celtics in the playoffs, and the Celtics had accounted for 5 of their 13 defeats during the regular season. Also, many people felt that Wilt would freeze in the big games. After all he had never taken his team to a championship —not even in college.

Wilt scoffed at such talk. "I beat the pants off Bill Russell in game after game," he told friends. "But his team beats my team because the Celtics have better players. If I had been playing for the Celtics, I would have won all those championships that the Celtics have won with Russell."

Some NBA players disagreed. "Wilt hates to get the ball in a close playoff game when his shot could mean the difference between winning or losing," said one player. "You can see it in his eyes; he doesn't want the ball."

In the opening round of the 1967 playoffs, however, Wilt was at his best. Blocking shots and pouring in points, he led the 76ers to victory over the Cincinnati Royals. Meanwhile, the Celtics defeated the New York Knicks in their opening round.

Boston and Philadelphia met in the semifinals. And the 76ers won the first three games. Now the Celtics were only one game away from total defeat. The Celtics' "five old men"—veterans Bailey Howell, Satch Sanders, K.C. and Sam Jones, and Russell—seemed exhausted after the long season. But young John Havlicek kept running, and the Celtics rallied to win the fourth game, 121–117. King Celtic was still alive.

Game five was played in Philadelphia.

Philadelphia's Hal Greer jars the ball loose from Boston's K.C. Jones as Bill Russell looks on.

From the opening tap, it was clear that Wilt was determined to stamp out these Celtics who had beaten him so often. He played "with murder glinting in both eyes," as one of his teammates put it.

But soon it was the Celtics who seemed to be on their way to a killing. Racing alongside Havlicek, they built up a 59–43 lead at one point. But then Wilt took over. He began to dunk, slam-dunk, and reverse-dunk. He ripped down rebounds. He shot passes to his teammates.

The 76ers closed in on the Celtics and finally grabbed the lead. After each 76er basket, the Philadelphia fans let out an explosive roar. The 76ers kept shooting, and the crowd kept shouting. The Celtics fell further and further behind. And finally, as coach Bill Russell stared mournfully from the bench, the Celtic streak of eight straight championships ended with a convincing 140–116 victory for the 76ers.

The 76ers weren't champions yet, however. They still had to beat the San Francisco Warriors in the finals. San Francisco had a 6-foot-11 center, Nate Thurmond, and the league's number one scorer, Rick Barry, who was averaging 35 points a game. But the 76ers had some big guns of their own. In five games they shot down the Warriors to win the 1967 NBA championship. After years of trying, Wilt had finally won the big one.

After winning the '67 championship, the jubilant 76ers douse Wilt with champagne.

Philadelphia fans were already predicting that a new 76er dynasty would rule the NBA. The 76ers were all young. And by now Wilt was unquestionably the league's best player. But Bill Russell and his captain, John Havlicek, told each other that the Celtics weren't finished yet.

28

UCLA: The Alcindor Years

The crowd packed into Pauley Pavilion let out a roar of astonishment. The UCLA Bruins had won the 1964 and 1965 NCAA championships, and many experts had picked them to win a third straight title in this 1965–66 season. But now, in a preseason exhibition game, they were being badly beaten—by the UCLA freshmen!

The freshman inflicting most of the damage was 7-foot-1 Lew Alcindor. Lew had been acclaimed as the greatest schoolboy basketball player of all time. At Power Memorial High School in New York he had stuffed in 50 and 60 points a game. "On

Freshman supercenter Lew Alcindor (33) gets the best of the UCLA varsity in an exhibition game.

defense, he can be as great as Russell," said college scouts. "On offense, he can be as great as Chamberlain."

Just about every college had tried to recruit Alcindor. But he had chosen UCLA, much to coach Wooden's delight. Now, as Wooden watched the big freshman, his delight turned to dismay. The coach feared that if the UCLA Bruins lost to the freshmen they might be drained of confidence before the regular season even began. Al-

ready Lew had scored 20 points for the freshmen, and the varsity was falling further and further behind.

Wooden watched as a freshman guard, Lucius Allen, dribbled the ball to the top of the foul circle. Allen stopped and looked at the pivot where Lew stood guarded by 6-foot-7 Mike Lynn, the varsity center. Allen lobbed the ball on a high arc toward Lew.

"I thought the ball was going to hit the roof of the building," Lynn said later. "But

Lew just reached up those arms, pulled it down, and dropped in a hook shot. Looking up at him, I felt like a little boy playing against his father."

Leaping higher than the backboard to pull down rebounds and dunk the ball into the hoop, Lew built up the freshman lead. Wooden signaled for the Monster—the UCLA full-court press that usually panicked opponents. But every time a UCLA freshman seemed to be trapped, he'd just heave the ball to Alcindor. When Lew grabbed the ball and held it high, the ball might as well have been on a mountain top. While the frustrated varsity players lunged at him, Lew coolly passed off to an open teammate—and the freshmen scored again.

Lew scored 31 points and pulled down 21 rebounds. And the freshmen shocked the varsity—and millions of fans across the country—by walloping the reigning NCAA champions, 75–60. As Wooden had feared,

Playing for the varsity in 1967, Lew took the Bruins to the NCAA championship.

that defeat seemed to deflate the Bruins. They finished the season with an 18–8 record and didn't even qualify for the NCAA tournament.

In the 1966–67 season Alcindor and the other members of the undefeated freshman team joined the varsity. Among the freshmen was guard Lucius Allen. According to Wooden, Allen "could be as great a little man as Lewis will be as a center." Then there was forward Lynn Shackleford, who shot with such precision that his teammates called him "The Machine." And guard Kenny Heitz was a stickler on defense. A holdover from last year's varsity was another guard, Mike Warren, one of the best playmakers in the game.

But when the Bruins met USC in the opening game of the season, all eyes were on "The Magnificent Seven-Footer," as the newspapers called Lew. The 19-year-old Lew wheeled to arch in hooks. He soared to tap in rebounds. He seemed to be playing on the lofty level of a second floor while everyone else played another game in the basement below. Scoring 56 points, a UCLA record, he helped the Bruins to an easy 105–90 victory.

Lew and the Bruins continued to shine for the rest of the season. Dropping in two of every three shots—a new college record—Alcindor averaged 29 points a game. The Bruins won every one of their 30 games. And in the NCAA tournament they overwhelmed Dayton, 79–64, to give John Wooden his third championship in four years.

In 1967–68 UCLA's starting five consisted of Alcindor, Allen, Warren, Shackleford, and Heitz. They picked up just where they'd left off the previous year. By midseason the Bruins had won 47 straight games, only 13 shy of the record set by Bill Russell and the University of San Francisco Dons in the 1950s.

To win their 48th in a row, the Bruins would have to overcome the University of

KAREEM ABDUL-JABBAR ▪close-up▪

The first-grade teacher frowned at the boy in the rear of the classroom. "You back there," she said sternly. "Please sit down."

"I am sitting down," the boy replied meekly, his knees jutting upward above the desk.

Even at six, Lewis Ferdinand Alcindor—later to be known as Kareem Abdul-Jabbar—stood out in a crowd. But it wasn't only his size that made Lew stand out. It was his color, too. Lew was a black child who grew up in a predominantly white neighborhood in New York. Both of Lew's parents were tall. His mother was a singer, his father a musician. But there weren't many jobs open to black musicians, so Mr. Alcindor got a job as a patrolman in the New York subways.

Mr. Alcindor always took his son to a black neighborhood for haircuts. When Lew was nine, he learned why. White barbers would not cut a black man's hair. Lew felt the sting of racial bigotry, and a fierce pride in his blackness began to burn inside him.

As a 6-foot-8 freshman, Lew entered Power Memorial High, a Catholic school in Manhattan. He was a good student—and a great basketball player. He pulled down more rebounds and scored more points than any player in New York schoolboy history. For three straight years he was named to the High School All-America team.

Every major college tried to recruit Lew, but he chose UCLA. When he arrived in California, however, Lew got an instant case of homesickness. He felt like an island in a sea of white faces. Lew believed that whites liked him only because he was a good athlete. So he turned his back on most of the white students. "I withdrew into myself to find myself," he later wrote. "I made no further attempts to integrate. I was consumed and obsessed by my interest in the black man, in black power, black pride, black courage."

In 1968, during his junior year at UCLA, Alcindor converted to the religion of Islam and adopted—privately at first and later publicly—the name Kareem Abdul-Jabbar. His new religion seemed to calm his troubled feelings about white people. "If racism messed up a lot of people who had to take it," he once wrote, "then it must also mess up those who had to dish it out. I did not want to be that kind of person."

In the UCLA dressing room he laughed and joked with his teammates. He enjoyed playing chess and became a masterful player. But in public he walked frozen-faced and stiff. He tried to ignore all those people below him with their stares and silly jokes about his height.

While he was at UCLA, college officials passed a rule outlawing the dunk shot. The rule was designed to make scoring more difficult for giants like Kareem. Yet he went on sinking six of every ten shots to become the most accurate shooter in college history. During his three varsity years at UCLA, he averaged over 26 points a game and led his team to three straight NCAA championships.

As a pro—first with the Milwaukee Bucks and later with the Los Angeles Lakers—he put in an average of 30 points a game to match the average of Wilt Chamberlain, the greatest scorer of all time. And he blocked shots that not even Bill Russell could have reached.

Throughout his career, Kareem earned the respect and admiration of coaches, teammates, and rivals. But no one was more impressed than Bill Russell, a man who knew all there was to know about the art of playing the pivot. "I think Kareem Abdul-Jabbar will be remembered as the greatest center ever," said Russell.

Houston. Houston had a winning streak of its own to protect. The team hadn't lost a game all season. A year earlier UCLA had defeated Houston in the NCAA semi-finals. But Houston's All-America center, Elvin "The Big E" Hayes, had outscored Lew in that game. Afterwards he'd bragged that he was a better center than Lew. And now he was determined to prove it.

Some 55,000 fans streamed into the Houston Astrodome to see this duel between the top-ranked Bruins and second-ranked Houston. It was the largest crowd ever to see a basketball game in the U.S. and the biggest for any indoor game (80,000 once watched the Globetrotters in an outdoor Berlin stadium). Millions more watched on TV as the two teams filed onto the floor.

Lew met the Big E for the center jump. "We're going to beat you bad," Hayes growled. A minute later the Big E soared high to toss in a one-hander. When Lew got the ball, he looked at the hoop and saw two hoops glimmering in the lights. A week earlier Lew's eyeball had been scratched in a game, and his vision was still blurry. But Lew had insisted on playing this game. He didn't want people to think he was afraid of Hayes.

But Lew couldn't focus on the hoop. Against Houston he took 18 shots, but only four went in. The Big E scored 39 points, and Houston snapped UCLA's winning streak with a 71–69 victory. "I proved it," The Big E exulted after the game. "I'm better than Alcindor!"

After that loss to Houston, UCLA didn't lose another game all season. In the semi-final round of the 1968 NCAA tournament UCLA and Houston met again. But now Houston, the highest-scoring team in the nation, was ranked number one, and UCLA was number two. Lew and the Bruins were looking to prove that UCLA was still the best team in the land.

Before the game began, coach John Wooden talked to Lynn Shackleford. "Stick

Elvin Hayes takes a shot on his way to leading Houston to a big victory over UCLA.

to Hayes," Wooden told the rangy forward. "Follow him into the seats if that's where he goes. Try to stop him from getting the ball. And when he does get the ball, stick so close to him that he can't get off a shot. If he goes around you, Lewis will be there to block his lay-up."

Wooden needn't have worried about Hayes. Alcindor was out for revenge, and this time his vision was clear. The big Bruin came out shooting. And Hayes, hemmed in by Shackelford, didn't score a single point for ten long minutes.

Early in the game, Wooden signaled for the Monster. The full-court press panicked the Houston players. Time after time they threw the ball into the hands of Bruins. At half time, UCLA led by 22 points, and the lead swelled to 44 points during the second half. The Big E put in only ten points as UCLA cruised to an easy 101–69 victory. Alcindor was the game's top scorer and rebounder. After the game a smiling Lew told reporters, "We just wanted to teach those people some manners."

UCLA went on to face North Carolina in the NCAA finals. This time Lew looped in 34 points, and UCLA won, 78–55. By the most lopsided score in any NCAA final, UCLA had won a second straight NCAA title and its fourth in five years.

Before the 1968–69 season, Lew's last, Lucius Allen dropped out of school and Mike Warren graduated. But Wooden had two tall, speedy sophomores to replace them—6-foot-6 Curtis Rowe and 6-foot-8 Sidney Wicks. The Bruins swept through their first 25 games without a defeat. Their last game of the season was against USC. The Trojans slowed down the action and took only sure, close-in shots. With only seconds to go they led, 46–44. Wicks lofted a jumper in an attempt to tie up the game, but the ball hit the front rim and bounced away. The jubilant Trojans leaped high off the floor. They had upset mighty UCLA.

The Bruins took their 25–1 record into the NCAA tournament. They breezed through the playoff rounds and met Purdue in the final. In his last game as a Bruin, Lew whisked in 37 points. UCLA coasted to a 92–72 victory . In Lew's three varsity years at UCLA, the Bruins had compiled an unbelievable 88–2 record. They had won three straight NCAA championships. Altogether UCLA had won five NCAA titles—more than any team ever. But now The Magnificent Seven-Footer was graduating, and John Wooden had to wonder if his team would ever win a sixth championship.

29

The Celtics: The Last Hurrah

"You guys yell at me when I slow down out there!" said Bill Russell to the Celtics at the start of the 1967–68 season. The 33-year-old player-coach knew that he often dragged in the last minutes of a game, and he wanted his teammates to spur him on. "The rest of me is thirty-three," he told them with a cackling laugh, "but my legs are a hundred."

Russell wasn't the only Celtic who was slowing down, however. Nearly all the other starters—Bailey Howell, Satch Sanders, and Sam Jones—were over 30, too. After eight straight years as NBA champions, the aging Celtics had been dethroned by Wilt Chamberlain and the Philadelphia 76ers in 1966–67.

Now sportswriters dismissed the Celtics as "over the hill," but Russell wasn't finished yet. He and young John Havlicek, the tireless Celtic captain, had a plan. From now on, Russell would save his strength and concentrate on defense for most of the game. But in the final minutes, egged on by his players, Russell would join the Celtic shooters in a closing rush for points.

Russell's plan worked pretty well. Havlicek and Bailey Howell did most of Boston's scoring. Together they tossed in about 40 points a game. And Russell blocked enough shots to make the Celtics one of the league's best defensive teams. Still, the Celtics finished only second in the NBA East, far behind the 76ers. In the playoffs the Celtics seemed likely to be gunned down by the 76ers.

The best-of-seven series between Boston and Philadelphia for the Eastern Division championship began in Philadelphia's shiny new Spectrum. Bill Russell always seemed to leap higher when he jumped against his old foe, Wilt Chamberlain, and this game was no exception. Russell pulled down one

Bill Russell dunks the ball during the 1968 NBA finals. Wilt Chamberlain (13) looks on.

rebound after another and blocked three of Wilt's hook shots. And Havlicek outran the surprised 76ers to steer the Celtics to an emphatic 127–118 victory.

"They'll be the ones who get surprised in our next game," Wilt said grimly after the defeat. And in the next game he and his teammates poured a blizzard of basketballs down around Celtic ears. The 76ers also went on to win the next two games. Leading three victories to one, the defending champions needed only one more victory to erase the Celtics.

The Celtics had their backs to the wall in game five. But again Russell flew high to block shots and seize rebounds. John Havlicek, Bailey Howell, and creaky-kneed Sam Jones tossed in one-handers, and the Celtics got their second victory, a 122–104 rout. The Celtics picked up another win in the sixth game to tie up the series at three games all.

The two teams met for another winner-take-all seventh game. Before the game got under way, the 32-year-old Chamberlain complained that his knees ached. And even some of the younger 76ers looked tired. "Havlicek's worn us out," one said. "He's like a perpetual motion machine."

The two tired teams struggled through the first half, neither able to jump out to a big lead. In the second half, with the game still close, Wilt suddenly seemed to lose his drive. He stood like a post and flicked the ball back to the 76ers whenever it was passed to him. With Wilt not shooting, the other 76ers rushed their shots—and missed. The Celtics began to pull ahead and scratched out a 100–96 victory.

The Celtics advanced to the finals, where they opposed the Los Angeles Lakers. The victory over the 76ers seemed to put new spring into the legs of the old Celtics. They bounced past the Lakers in six games to win their ninth championship in ten years and their tenth in the past twelve—a record that had no equal in American sports.

109

During the 1969 playoffs, John Havlicek (right) gets caught in the cross fire between teammate Bailey Howell and Laker Elgin Baylor . . .

That championship seemed a last-gasp victory for the gallant old Celtics. At the start of the 1968–69 season almost everyone was counting Boston out. The Los Angeles Lakers were expected to run away from the rest of the league. "The Lakers may never lose a game," some fans predicted. "They'll be the Celtics of the future."

The Lakers had an all-star line-up. Two of their starters, Jerry West and Elgin Baylor, would eventually become the third- and fourth-highest scorers of all time. And to top it all off, they'd just acquired the game's

number one scorer—big Wilt himself—in a trade. "This is the greatest bunch of scorers ever assembled," said Laker owner Jack Kent Cooke.

The Lakers would have some new competition, however. By 1968 the NBA had expanded from 10 to 14 teams. The Milwaukee Bucks had joined the Eastern Division, and the Phoenix Suns, Seattle Super-Sonics, and San Diego Rockets played in the West.

All-Americas came into the league and became instant stars. In his rookie season,

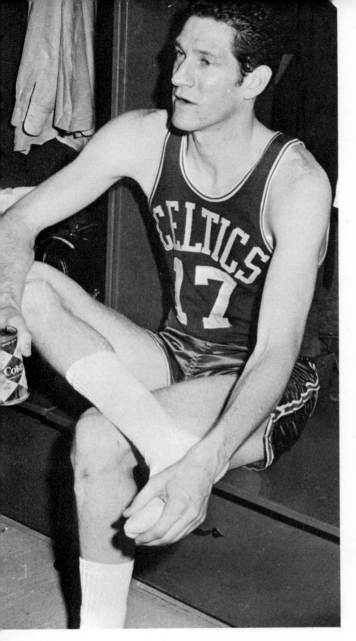

. . . then takes a well-earned rest in the Celtics' locker room.

San Diego's Elvin Hayes led the NBA in scoring. And Baltimore's Wes Unseld, a burly defense specialist, was the Rookie of the Year and the league's Most Valuable Player. The new teams and new superstars drew more and more fans to the NBA, and attendance soared to almost four and a half million.

The face of the pro player had changed as the face of America changed. This was a time of long-haired students and campus protests against the war in Vietnam. Up to now all NBA players, by personal preference or on orders of their coaches, sported crew-cuts or short hair and clean-shaven faces. But now, when "doing your own thing" was the guiding precept for many young people, players had mustaches, beards, long side-burns, and bushy Afros or shaggy mops that curled modishly around their ears.

The team standings at the end of that 1968–69 season showed just how much things had changed in the NBA. Boston finished way down in fourth place in the NBA East with a 48–35 record. Because the league had expanded, however, that fourth-place finish was good enough to qualify the Celtics for the playoffs.

The 35-year-old Russell's playing legs were shot. He had played all year on pure instinct and guts. Only the shooting of John Havlicek and Bailey Howell, with help from subs Sam Jones and Don Nelson, had kept the Celtics' head above water. In this play-off the tired old Celtics seemed sure to sink.

But the scent of another championship seemed to rouse Russell for one last effort. In the opening round, he played like the Bill Russell of the '50s. The Celtics swept by the 76ers, then defeated the young and strong New York Knicks in the semi-finals to enter another NBA final.

This time they met the powerful Lakers. Pitted against Wilt Chamberlain, as he'd been so many times during this decade, Bill Russell managed to contain his old foe. But Jerry West and Elgin Baylor couldn't be stopped, and the Lakers easily won the first two games.

The Celtics scrapped back, winning the next two games to tie the series. The Lakers went ahead again with a 117–104 victory in game five, but the Celtics wouldn't give up. They won the sixth game, 99–90, to tie the series at three victories apiece.

Game seven was not only the final game of the series, it was the final game of Bill Russell's career. The Celtic superstar was retiring, and he wanted one more championship before he left. The game was just

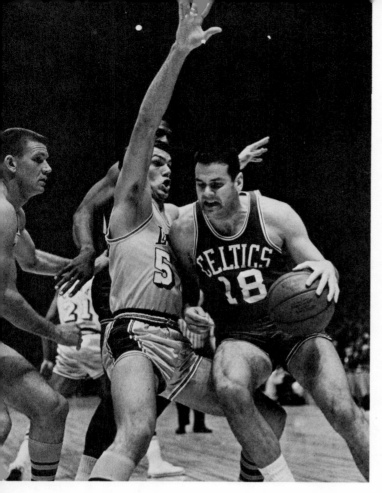

Howell muscles his way past Laker Dennis Hamilton and is called for an offensive foul.

as important to the Lakers, however. They were playing in their sixth NBA final in eight years, and they'd never yet won a championship.

Both teams played as hard as they could, and the lead shifted time after time. Late in the game, Celtic supersub Don Nelson lofted a shot that hit the front rim, bounced high into the air, and dropped through the nets. That basket turned out to be crucial. Boston won the game by only two points, 108–106. The Celtics ran proudly off the Los Angeles court, champs once again.

That was Bill Russell's last game as a Celtic player and coach. The dynasty that had begun when he, Cousy, and Sharman led the Celtics to their first championship way back in 1957 would end, with this victory, their 11th, in 1969. Some of those championships were won on lucky bounces —the Selvy shot that didn't go in, the Nelson shot that did. But all of those championships were won with rare skill and even rarer courage.

30

Birth of the ABA

While fans flocked to see Lew Alcindor, Bill Russell, and Wilt Chamberlain in the mid-1960s, a long-faced young black man played alone on a windy schoolyard in Pittsburgh. Each afternoon he tossed a basketball at a rusty iron hoop. When he missed a shot, he'd chase after the ball, hands stuffed into his pockets to keep them warm.

His name was Connie Hawkins. In 1960 he had been considered one of the greatest schoolboy basketball players in New York City. Now, six years later, he was 24, jobless, and near penniless.

The 6-foot-7 Hawkins had played for Brooklyn's Boys High. Driving toward the basket like an express train, he'd scored 40

and 50 points a game. And he was almost impossible to beat at rebounding.

College scouts descended on the Brooklyn ghetto where Connie lived. From 200 offers Connie chose the University of Iowa. But during Connie's freshman year, New York City detectives came to Iowa and asked him to return to the city. There he was questioned by a district attorney.

The D.A. was investigating gambler Jack Molinas, a former basketball player, who had been caught giving gifts to high school and college players. Boys such as Connie, who had taken small gifts from Molinas, were asked if they had thrown games or shaved points. "What could we do for the fixers?" asked Roger Brown, another player who was questioned with Connie. "We were still in high school."

But college presidents feared a new basketball scandal that would turn fans away from their games. To protect themselves, the colleges tossed players such as Connie and Roger Brown off the campus —without a trial or any real evidence of wrongdoing.

Connie returned to Brooklyn, distraught and desperate. He had hoped that his basketball talent would lift him out of his ghetto and its poverty. Now his future seemed bleak. No college or NBA team would even talk to him.

Hawkins became a basketball vagabond. For a while he toured with the Harlem Globetrotters. Then he signed to play for a Pittsburgh team in a pro league that soon collapsed. By 1966 he was living on the $25 he earned weekends playing for a team called the Harlem Wizards. And on weekdays he tossed a basketball alone in a cold Pittsburgh schoolyard.

Then one afternoon in 1967 Connie got a phone call that changed his life. A new pro league, to be called the American Basketball Association, was being formed. Connie was offered $15,000 a year to play for the Pittsburgh Pipers in the new ABA, and he accepted gladly.

For much more money the ABA had signed several NBA stars, notably Cliff Hagan, the former St. Louis Hawk. And with fistfuls of dollars, it had lured some 1967 All-Americas away from the NBA. The best of these were Kentucky's Lou Dampier and New Mexico's Mel Daniels.

The ABA started the 1967–68 season with 11 teams. Its commissioner was George Mikan. The new league used a flashy red, white, and blue ball. And it had a rule that brought fans to their feet. If a player arched in a shot from beyond 25 feet, the basket counted for three points. "The three-point play," explained a now scholarly looking

After being banned from the NBA, an unhappy Connie Hawkins played semi-pro ball in 1962.

Mikan, "gives to basketball the same thunderclap excitement that the home run gives to baseball."

Immediately two ABA teams—the Indiana Pacers and the Kentucky Colonels—drew crowds of 5,000 and more. That equaled the attendance at many NBA games. But the other nine ABA teams played before rows of empty seats.

"We need name stars," Mikan told the ABA owners. "We have got to outbid the NBA for their stars and the famous All-Americas."

The ABA did have one star—Connie Hawkins. In that first season, he led the league in scoring, flipping in 26 points a

113

In 1968 the ABA gave Hawkins a chance to play pro ball. Here he scores for the Pittsburgh Pipers.

game. And only Minnesota's Mel Daniels pulled down more rebounds. Led by Hawkins, the Pittsburgh Pipers finished first in their division, then vanquished the New Orleans Buccaneers to win the first ABA championship.

"Connie," said Roger Brown of Indiana, "can do everything. He would be a star in the NBA, and he is the best all-around player in this league."

But Connie was not the superstar that the ABA needed. First of all, he was black, and the TV networks thought a white high scorer would attract more viewers. Connie, moreover, was quiet and shied away from the spotlight. But before the 1968–69 season began, the ABA found the superstar it was seeking. He was blond and cocky, and he dressed fashionably in the latest mod clothes. Most important, he could do all the things on a basketball court that Connie Hawkins could do—leap to stuff the ball, drive to the hoop, float one-handers from outside. A muscled 6-foot-7 forward, his name was Rick Barry.

In 1965 Barry had joined the NBA's San Francisco Warriors after All-America high-scoring years at the University of Miami. As a rookie, he'd led the Warriors in scoring with 25 points a game. The next year he led the whole NBA with 35 a game.

Rick drove toward the basket with dipsy-doodling moves that shook off defenders. From outside he corkscrewed into the air to toss in jumpers from seemingly impossible angles. And his foul shooting was almost perfect. With an old-fashioned, knee-dipping, underhanded shot, he shoveled in almost nine of every ten of his free throws.

"I can sink fouls blindfolded," he once boasted to his Warrior teammates. When the players hooted, Rick shut his eyes and tossed six of ten throws through the hoop.

Six of ten wasn't good enough for Rick, however. "That basket is an inch-and-a-half too high," he said.

Grinning, the players measured the basket. To their astonishment, they saw that Rick was right: the basket was exactly an inch-and-a-half too high.

After leading the NBA in scoring in 1967, Rick accepted an offer of $75,000 a year to jump to the ABA's Oakland Oaks. Rick's father-in-law, his former Miami coach, became the coach of the Oaks.

The NBA Warriors tried to stop Rick from jumping to the new league. They appealed to a judge. But the judge ruled that if Rick sat out one season, he could then play for whomever he wished.

Rick, who wanted to be a TV or movie actor, spent the next year (1967–68) broadcasting the Oakland games. He broadcast very little happy news, though. His father-in-law's team wound up with the worst record in the new league.

The next season, Alex Hannum took over as coach of the Oaks, and Rick joined the team. With Rick leading the way, the Oaks flashed to victory in 14 of their first 16 games. Rick rammed in a league-leading 35 points a game and attracted thousands of fans to the ABA games. Some 9,000 came to see him in Indianapolis, and more than 13,000 turned out for a game in Louisville —an ABA record.

Rick put on quite a show for the crowds. He flung punches at opponents, ranted at referees, and thumbed his nose at fans. Some people loved him, and some people hated him. But almost everyone wanted to see Rick Barry. "When Rick comes to town," said one delighted ABA owner, "the sparks fly. The league needs ten Rick Barrys."

Rick was almost too much of a good thing, however. He and the Oaks were so good that fans became bored watching them overwhelm the competition. As the season progressed, fewer and fewer fans came to see them play. "Barry will score a lot of points, and Oakland will win," fans said. "So why bother going to see the inevitable?"

It came as no surprise to anyone when the Oaks ran off with the 1969 championship. But for the Oakland owner, victory had been costly. He had lost so much money that he decided to sell the Oaks to a group of businessmen, who moved the team to Washington, D.C.

Other owners were worried. The ABA had lost its first star, Connie Hawkins. Connie had filed a million-dollar suit against the NBA for barring him from its league. As

Rick Barry, the Oaks' "Golden Boy," brought a lot of glamour—and talent—to the ABA.

part of the settlement Connie had finally been allowed to join the NBA. One star— even one as great as Rick Barry—just wasn't enough to keep the ABA alive.

Getting new stars was easier said than done, however—and a lot more expensive. The new league was still engaged in a bidding war with the NBA, and salaries in both leagues were climbing higher every day.

31

The Pacers Set the Pace

The white check slid across the table. It stopped in front of Lew Alcindor, who now preferred to be called Kareem Abdul-Jabbar. The former UCLA superstar glanced down at the check. Across its face were stamped the words "One million dollars."

Kareem was seated at a table in a room of a Manhattan skyscraper. Around him, on this spring day in 1969, sat Kareem's lawyers and several owners of American Basketball Association teams. The ABA owners had pooled their resources and dipped into their treasuries for the million dollars. It was Kareem's if he would sign to play for an ABA team.

"Is that your final offer?" Kareem asked coolly. The owners said yes. Kareem nodded and said he would let them know.

But Kareem had made up his mind. He'd already been offered the same amount of money by the NBA's Milwaukee Bucks. And he wanted to play in the NBA. "As a kid," he explained later, "I used to practice shooting like Wilt Chamberlain. I even used to comb my hair like Wilt. I always wanted to play against him—but I won't if I go to the ABA."

ABA owners winced when Abdul-Jabbar signed with Milwaukee. They had failed to sign the one player who could have made the ABA nearly as well thought of as the NBA. But if the ABA didn't have an individual star to compare with Kareem, before the 1969–70 season ended it would claim to have a whole team that was as good, if not better, than any in the NBA.

That ABA team was the Indiana Pacers. The Pacers had the best shot blocker and rebounder in the league—a brawny 6-foot-9 center named Mel Daniels, the former

Pacer star Roger Brown gets tangled up with Los Angeles's Cliff Anderson.

Minnesota star. And 6-foot-5 Roger Brown was a great shooter, especially when he unloosed 25-foot bombs that were good for three points in the ABA. Also piling up points for the Pacers were guards Freddie Lewis and Billy Keller and a bruising forward named Bob Netolicky.

But Indiana was more than just a collection of stars; it was a team. Working together on offense and defense, the Pacers dominated the league. They finished the season with a 59–25 record, then breezed through the playoffs to meet the Los Angeles Stars in the finals.

Roger Brown went on a real shooting spree against the Stars. In one game he put in 53 points, an ABA record at that time. And in another he scored 45, including seven three-pointers. The other Pacers pitched in to defeat Los Angeles, four games to two, and win their first ABA crown.

In the 1970–71 season, standing-room-only crowds filled the State Fairgrounds Coliseum in Indianapolis to watch the Pacers defend their championship. The crowds at Pacer games were the largest, and most avid, in the league. Dressed in Pacer T-shirts, fans drove to the games in cars emblazoned with Pacer bumper stickers. Before the games, they attended Pacer parties. And at those parties, the fans sometimes speculated about what might have happened if their team had played against the great NBA teams of the past—the Boston Celtics or the Minneapolis Lakers. Needless to say, in the fans' imaginary games, the Pacers seldom, if ever, came out the losers.

Ex-Celtic Bill Sharman didn't dispute the fans. Sharman was now the coach of the Utah Stars. (The Los Angeles ABA team had moved to Utah at the start of the season.) As Sharman saw it, "Roger Brown could be an outstanding forward in the NBA. And Mel Daniels is as good a rebounder as any in the NBA." But shortly after Sharman made that comment, his Utah Stars shocked the Pacers by eliminating them in the playoff semi-finals. The Stars' 6-foot-9 Zelmo Beaty, a former NBA center, outplayed the younger Mel Daniels. Then Zelmo and the Stars defeated Kentucky in the finals and became the fourth team in four years to wear the ABA crown.

The Pacer owners were determined to win back that title. Before the 1971–72 season began, they waved their checkbooks at one

Mel Daniels pulls down a rebound against the Stars in the 1970 ABA championship.

of the greatest college players in the country. His name was George McGinnis. Big and strong, George stood 6-foot-8 and weighed 240 pounds of solid muscle. Yet he was as quick as a rabbit. Playing for Indiana University, he'd led the Big Ten Conference both in scoring and rebounding. The Pacers offered George a three-year contract for $350,000.

There was only one problem. George was just a sophomore. College coaches screamed that the pros were "kidnapping" their best players, and NBA owners denounced the

117

ABA for trying to sign McGinnis. But George decided to quit college and join the Pacers. He figured that by the time he graduated from college, the war between the two leagues might be over and pro salaries would plummet.

Veteran NBA players lifted their eyebrows when they heard how much this Indiana college boy was getting. Proven stars such as Oscar Robertson made it clear that they thought they were worth at least as much money as an untested rookie. In fact, the Big O demanded—and got—a raise to $250,000 a year. Pro basketball players had now become the highest-paid athletes in any team sport.

As far as the Pacers were concerned, however, McGinnis was worth every penny of his huge salary. Although he made his share of rookie mistakes, George piled up an impressive number of rebounds and points in his first pro year. "When big George goes to the hoop with his size and speed," said one player, "he carries four or five guys with him by the vacuum he creates."

Led by McGinnis and Roger Brown, the Pacers easily qualified for the 1972 playoffs. They overcame the Utah Stars in the semifinals, then faced the New York Nets in the finals. Starring for the Nets was Rick Barry, who had been traded to New York in 1970. But New York was no match for Indiana. The Pacers took the series, four games to two, to win their second championship in three years.

The following season (1972–73) George whirled and drove for 27 points a game, second highest in the league. Again the Pacers rose to the ABA finals. There they met a tough Kentucky Colonels team sparked by three of Adolph Rupp's former All-Americas—center Dan Issel and guards Lou Dampier and Darel Carrier.

Kentucky and Indiana battled through the first six games, each winning three. In the seventh and final game George fired in

Signed by the Pacers for $350,000, George McGinnis had plenty to smile about.

27 points to give the Pacers their second straight ABA title and their third in four years.

Pacer fans cried "Dynasty!" and predicted that their team would go on to win more championships than the Celtics. ABA fans looked forward to a "Super Bowl" pitting the ABA champions against the NBA champs. But there'd be no such interleague game—and no Pacer dynasty.

32

UCLA: The Walton Gang

Artis Gilmore, the Jacksonville giant, wheeled toward the hoop, the ball clutched at the end of a long arm. The 7-foot-2 Gilmore hooked a short shot from behind his ear. Up from the floor soared UCLA's 6-foot-8 Sidney Wicks, who easily flicked away the ball.

Watching UCLA battle the University of Jacksonville in this 1970 NCAA tournament final, the huge crowd let out a surprised roar. The Bruins were looking very strong. Yet at the beginning of the 1969–70 season, few fans had expected them to get this far. Lew Alcindor, now known as Kareem Abdul-Jabbar, had graduated, and John Wooden had no seven-foot skyscraper to replace him. The UCLA dynasty seemed sure to fall.

Although he no longer had a real supercenter, Wooden had something almost as effective—a trio of rebounding shot-blockers. The big three included a 6-foot-9 center, Steve Patterson, and two rangy forwards, 6-foot-6 Curtis Rowe and 6-foot-8 Sidney Wicks. Wicks and Rowe had grown up on ghetto playgrounds in Los Angeles and brought some dazzling schoolyard moves to UCLA.

Wooden also had two fast guards in John Vallely and Henry Bibby. The Bruins called Vallely "Money Man" because he hit so often late in games. And Bibby was a great outside shooter. "He can hit from farther out than any player I have ever coached," said Wooden.

Although they lacked the height of Wooden's previous teams, the 1969–70 Bruins had made a strong showing during the regular season. UCLA had finished with

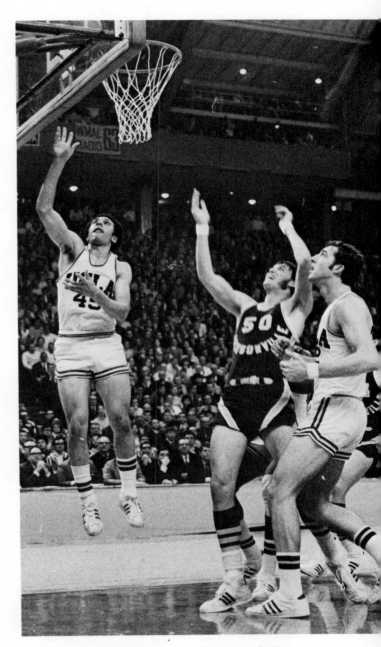

Speedy Henry Bibby gets to the hoop before his Jacksonville rivals.

a 27–2 record to qualify for the NCAA tournament. In the playoffs they'd had little trouble beating Long Beach State (88–65) and Utah State (101–79).

But now in the NCAA finals the Bruins were facing two seven-footers—Artis Gilmore and Pembrook Burrows. Sidney Wicks, who barely reached Gilmore's chin, was assigned the unenviable job of stopping Jacksonville's highest scorer. And as the crowd gasped in amazement, Wicks proceeded to get the job done.

Early in the game Gilmore lofted a one-hander toward the hoop. But Sidney flew up and swatted the shot aside. Then Gilmore turned for a hook shot, and Sidney batted that away. Later Wicks deflected a jumper . . . and then another. Altogether he blocked five shots by Gilmore and came out of that game with a new name—"Super Sidney." And the UCLA Bruins, 80–69 winners, came out of the game with their fourth straight NCAA title, their sixth in seven years.

After the game, the jubilant Bruins celebrated in the winners' dressing room. The happiest Bruin of all was Curtis Rowe, who'd led his team on offense with 19 points. "Every time somebody mentions three titles in a row, they say Lew did it," Rowe told reporters. "Now we just proved that four other men on the team could play basketball —with the best of them."

The following season (1970–71) the Bruins boasted a 25–1 record. Their only defeat was inflicted by Notre Dame on the Irish home court at South Bend. Again the Bruins qualified for the NCAA tournament, and again they went all the way. In the finals UCLA beat Villanova, 68–62, to win its fifth national title in a row.

Fans compared Wooden's UCLA dynasty to Red Auerbach's Celtic dynasty. The Celtics had won 11 NBA championships from 1957 to 1969. The Bruins hadn't won that many yet, but in a way their achievements were even more impressive than the Celtics'. After all, Auerbach had been able to keep his players for years—until their legs gave way. But John Wooden could keep his Bruins for a maximum of three years. Then, at their peak as college players, they'd grad-

UCLA's Sidney Wicks outjumps 7-foot-2 Artis Gilmore to pull down a rebound in the 1970 NCAA championship final against Jacksonville.

120

Big Bill Walton (left) took over where Lew Alcindor left off, leading UCLA to two more championships and a record-breaking winning streak.

uate. Almost every season Wooden had to find a replacement for one, two, or more starters. At the beginning of the 1971–72 season, Wooden had to find just about a whole new team. Of the previous year's champions, only Henry Bibby was still in school. And he was now a senior. But Wooden wasn't worried. Coming up from the freshman team was a 6-foot-11, red-haired, freckle-faced center, whom Wooden compared to Bill Russell. "He can go higher than Russell to block shots and get rebounds," the coach said. "And unlike Russell, when Bill was in college, this boy can score points."

The young giant's name was Bill Walton, and for the next three years that name would mean UCLA to fans across the nation. In fact, the Bruins would become known as "The Walton Gang."

The 1971–72 Bruins won all 30 of their games. Walton tossed in as many as 35 points a game while hammering down a slew of shots by opposing centers. "You know, I sometimes wish Alcindor was back," one coach admitted after his team was demolished by UCLA.

UCLA wasn't a one-man team, however. Henry Bibby exerted a steadying influence on the young Bruins and was as effective as ever with his long-range bombs. And sophomore Keith Wilkes, an eel of a forward, slithered through the tightest defenses.

In the NCAA finals against Florida State, Walton put in 24 points, Wilkes 23, and Bibby 18 to pace the Bruins to their sixth straight championship.

The Gang went right on winning in 1972–73. UCLA stretched its winning streak to 50 games, then 55 as it closed in on the record of 60 set by Bill Russell's San Francisco Dons in the 1950s. In January 1973, the Bruins tied the record with a victory over Loyola and broke it the next day by beating Notre Dame.

The Bruins finished the season still undefeated. In the 1973 NCAA finals they took on Memphis State. In the greatest performance of his college career Walton scored 44 points and blocked a dozen shots to lead UCLA to its seventh straight NCAA championship.

Walton and his Gang came back for one last season in 1973–74. They continued to stretch out their winning streak—70 games . . . 80 games . . . 85 games in a row

Walton soars above the crowd to score against Memphis State in the 1973 NCAA finals.

without a defeat. By January of 1974 they had won 88 straight games. Not one member of this Walton Gang knew what it felt like to lose in a UCLA uniform.

On January 19, 1974, UCLA arrived at South Bend to play Notre Dame. It was in this same arena that the Bruins had last been defeated—on January 23, 1971, three years earlier.

Millions of fans across the nation sat in front of their TV sets to see if the Irish could beat the Bruins again. Notre Dame students filled the cavernous arena with an ear-splitting racket as they tried to unnerve Walton and the Bruins. But Bill would not be distracted. He led the Bruins in scoring, and with only three minutes to go UCLA was comfortably ahead, 70–59.

Suddenly the Irish came alive. Notre Dame's John Shumate, Adrian Dantley, and Gary Brokaw closed the gap with a barrage of shots. With 30 seconds remaining, the Irish rushed to within a point of UCLA, 70–69. Then Notre Dame's Dwight Clay popped a one-hander from the side, and the ball swirled through the net. Now Notre Dame led, 71–70.

UCLA swept downcourt with the ball. A Bruin let fly a shot, which hit the rim and bounced off. Bill Walton grabbed the rebound, and threw it back up. The ball hit the rim and popped off. Another Bruin frantically tried to tap it back up. Suddenly the buzzer cut through the din. The ecstatic Irish had just pulled off one of the biggest upsets ever. They had beaten UCLA, 71–70, and ended college basketball's longest winning streak.

A week later the Bruins exacted a measure of revenge with a 94–75 rout of the Irish at Pauley Pavilion. But then UCLA lost two games in a row. Not since 1966 had a UCLA team lost two games in a row. And in the semi-finals of the 1974 NCAA tournament, the Bruins were eliminated by North Carolina.

Most of the Walton Gang graduated that June, and Wooden again had to rebuild a team almost from scratch. And this time there was no superstar coming up from the freshman ranks. The Bruins opened the 1974–75 season with Andre McCarter and Pete Trgovich at guard, Dave Meyers and Marques Johnson at forward, and 6-foot-9 Richard Washington in the pivot. Like Wooden's first champion team, in 1964, this was a team of "no-names."

Patiently and methodically, Wooden steered his team through the season. Like a puppet master, he pulled invisible strings that slowed his players down or sped them up. "When you play John Wooden," said an opposing coach, "he makes you play the game that's best for his side."

The no-name Bruins came through with a surprising 29–3 record. They climbed to the semi-finals of the 1975 NCAA tournament, where they met a team from the University of Louisville. With seconds to go, Louisville led the Bruins, 74–73. But Richard Washington whisked in a shot, and UCLA held on to win, 75–74. Once more a grinning John Wooden had brought the Bruins to another NCAA final.

After the game Wooden, who had suffered a mild heart attack a year earlier, told his players that this next game would be his last. "I'm bowing out," he told them. "I don't want to. I have to."

"Win this one for Wooden," the UCLA players urged each other before the championship final against Kentucky. And that's just what they did with a 92–85 victory over the Wildcats. John Wooden had his 10th NCAA trophy in 12 years.

In his 27 years at UCLA the Bruins had won 620 games and lost 147. That was about eight victories in every ten games. No other coach in any major sport—neither Vince Lombardi in football nor Casey Stengel in baseball—had ever maintained such a high percentage of victories. When he retired in 1975 John Wooden was the "winningest" coach ever.

33
Knick Smarts

"Dee-fense (clap-clap) . . . Dee-fense (clap-clap) . . . Dee-fense . . ."

That rhythmic chant filled Madison Square Garden during the 1970 NBA play-off finals. In this fifth game of the championship series, New York Knickerbocker fans were calling on their team to hold back big Wilt Chamberlain and his Los Angeles Lakers.

The two teams had struggled through the first four games of the seven-game series, winning two apiece. But now in game five

the Lakers were ahead by ten points, and the Knicks seemed powerless to stop them. The Knicks' bulky center, the 6-foot-8 Willis Reed, had just fallen and injured his hip. Reed was finished for the night—and probably the rest of the series. Without Reed there to block Chamberlain's shots, the Lakers were threatening to break the game wide open. As Reed limped off to the locker room, the Knicks huddled around their coach, Red Holzman.

In the 1940s Red had played at CCNY

In game five of the 1970 playoffs, Knick center Willis Reed battles Wilt Chamberlain (left), *then limps off the court* (right) *with an injured hip.*

for coach Nat Holman, the Original Celtic. Nat had taught Red the Original Celtic style of basketball, and Red had taught it to the Knicks. On offense, Holzman's Knicks weaved around the basket trying to shake their defenders. When a Knick broke free, a teammate would feed him the ball for a short jumper or an easy lay-up. On defense, the Knicks worked as a team, switching off and helping each other whenever necessary. The Knicks had no soaring leaper like Bill Russell and no supershooter like Jerry West. But what they did have, New Yorkers claimed, was "the smarts." They played a thinking man's game.

Of course, the Knicks had excellent players of their own, starting with their captain, Willis Reed. At 6-foot-8 and 250 pounds, Willis looked like a fireplug next to a telephone pole when he stood next to the NBA's taller centers. But Willis was as strong as a wrestler. He knew how to push and shove the giants away from the hoop, forcing them to shoot from outside their normal range. On offense the burly Willis was as agile as a smaller man, darting by much bigger centers to toss in hooks and lay-ups.

The Knicks also had a ball-stealing guard who had the quick hands of a pickpocket. His name was Walt Frazier, and he was one of the best all-around players in the league. New York's other starters were Dick Barnett, a guard, and Dave DeBusschere and Bill Bradley, two forwards. All three could hit from outside.

Because Knick ballhandlers always looked for the open man, the team had no truly outstanding scorer. Walt Frazier and Willis Reed averaged around 21 points a game while Barnett, Bradley, and DeBusschere put in around 15. "We have no all-stars," Red Holzman said with pride. "But we have the most balanced offense in the history of the NBA."

That balanced offense—and ball-stealing defense—had won 18 straight games for the Knicks in this 1969–70 season, a new NBA record. The Knicks had finished first in the NBA East and climbed all the way to the playoff finals. But as the Knicks huddled around Holzman in this fifth game, their fans feared that without Reed the Knicks were doomed to defeat.

Holzman wasn't about to quit now. He'd already come up with a plan. "They'll try to get the ball in to Chamberlain," he told his Knicks. "You know what to do. Try to cut off their passes to Chamberlain."

The Knicks trotted back onto the court. A grim-faced Dave DeBusschere, only 6-foot-6, was assigned to guard Wilt. Play resumed. The Lakers brought down the ball. And just as Red had predicted, they tried to get it to Wilt. But when a Laker lobbed a pass to Chamberlain, the Knicks intercepted the ball and put it up for a two-pointer. Again the Lakers brought up the ball and tried to feed it to Wilt. Again the ball was grabbed by a Knick. And again the Knicks scored.

The Lakers went on steering the ball to Chamberlain, and the Knicks went on intercepting the passes and converting them into New York baskets. Meanwhile, the Lakers were so intent on hitting Chamberlain that they ignored their other high-scoring star, Jerry West. With so many Knicks concentrating on Wilt, West was often open for an outside shot. But the Lakers just didn't see him. Chamberlain and West, Los Angeles's best scorers, got only four baskets in the second half, and the Knicks surged ahead to a 107–100 victory. Even without Willis Reed, the Knicks had beaten Chamberlain and the Lakers.

The Knicks now led the final series, three games to two. They needed just one more victory to win the championship. But Willis Reed was still sidelined when the sixth game began. And this time the Knicks couldn't do without him. The Lakers, embarrassed by their poor showing in game five, pulled out all the stops and thumped the Knicks

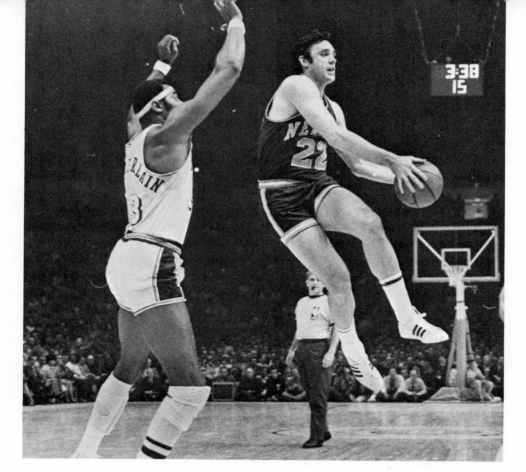

With Reed out of the line-up for game six, the Knicks had to rely on burly forward Dave DeBusschere.

soundly, 135–113. No one knew whether Reed would be able to play in the seventh and final game. As the teams trotted onto the floor for their pre-game warm-ups, Knick fans anxiously searched for Willis's bulky figure. They groaned when they didn't see him, and the Lakers breathed a sign of relief.

But seconds before the opening tap-off, a sudden roar shook the Garden. Willis Reed had just stepped out of a doorway and onto the court. Willis' hip still ached, but he didn't want the Lakers to know he was in pain. He made himself walk with a firm step. Reed joined the Knicks and flipped in a couple of practice shots while the crowd continued to cheer.

The game began. On the very first play, Willis broke away from his man and sprang free under the hoop. Frazier whipped the ball to him, and Reed floated in a soft jumper. The crowd screamed for more, and a minute later Reed whisked in another

jumper. The Lakers stared in amazement. They had expected the Knicks' big man to be limping.

Reed didn't stay in the game long. He was in too much pain. But he'd done his job. Those four quick points had lifted the Knicks' spirits and totally demoralized the Lakers. "I was turned up so high, I never did come down," Walt Frazier said after the game.

When Reed left the floor early in the second quarter, the Knicks had a comfortable lead. They held on to it for the rest of the game and coasted to a 113–99 victory. For the first time since they'd joined the old Basketball Association of America back in 1946, the Knicks were league champions.

With a team of young players, the Knicks hoped to succeed the Celtics as the new dynasty in the NBA. But in the years to come, the Knicks—and a lot of other champs—would find that NBA crowns were made to be knocked off.

34

Olympic Upset

Another basket for the Russians. The wall-to-wall crowd at the Olympic Stadium in Munich, Germany, began to cheer in a dozen different languages. With only ten minutes remaining in this final game for the 1972 Olympic basketball championship,

Ed Ratleff (15) attempts to block a shot by a Russian player during the 1972 Olympics.

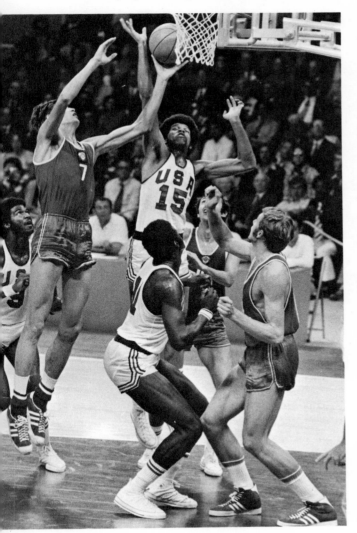

Russia now led the United States, 38–28. The fans sensed that they were about to witness one of the biggest upsets in the history of the games.

Up to now, no U.S. team had ever lost an Olympic basketball game. A U.S. team had won the gold medal at the first Olympics in 1936. And in the six Olympics since then, U.S. teams had won six more gold medals. Probably the best of those teams had been the 1960 squad, featuring Jerry Lucas, Jerry West, and Oscar Robertson, which had defeated Brazil, 90–63, in Rome. In 1964, at Tokyo, a U.S. team led by UCLA's Walt Hazzard and Princeton's Bill Bradley had beaten Russia, 73–59. And in 1968, at Mexico City, a guard named Jo Jo White and forward named Spencer Haywood had been the driving force behind the Americans' 65–50 victory over Yugoslavia.

"But it's only a matter of time until we lose in the Olympics," the U.S. basketball coach, Hank Iba, had warned before the start of the 1972 games. "Look at the Russian team. It's a national team. The players have been together for more than seven hundred games since the last Olympics. Our team was put together only a few months ago."

The Russian players had another edge. They were familiar with international rules. American college players weren't used to the speedier pace of international basketball, which required teams to shoot within 30 seconds.

But the 1972 U.S. team had a couple of advantages of its own—namely, guard Doug Collins of Illinois and forward Tom Mc-Millen of Maryland. The two All-Americas had led their team through the playoff rounds

In the Olympic playoffs, Doug Collins (5) puts up a shot against Czechoslovakia's Zdenek Kos.

without a single defeat. But now, in the finals, the Russians seemed to be getting the best of the Americans.

The Russians were playing a shrewd game. Whenever an American seemed to have a clear shot at the basket, the Russians would try to foul him. (Under international rules, if a player was fouled before he took a shot, he got possession of the ball, but no free throw.) Those intentional fouls reduced the Americans' scoring. The Russians built up a 38–28 lead.

The desperate Hank Iba signaled for a full-court press. The Americans swarmed all over the Russian ballhandler, who promptly committed a turnover. Every time the Russians got the ball, the U.S. continued its harrying defense. Millions of Americans back home, who were watching the game via satellite TV, cheered as their team began to make a comeback. With less than a minute remaining, the U.S. closed the gap to a single point, 49–48.

Then Doug Collins drove to the basket and was fouled in the act of shooting. He was awarded two free throws. Doug coolly threw in the first shot to tie up the game, 49–all. Just as he put up the second shot, the buzzer sounded. No one seemed to know what the buzzer signified. No one seemed to care either. Collins's shot had gone in, and the U.S. now led, 50–49.

There were only three seconds left on the clock as the Russians tossed the ball in-bounds. An American deflected the pass. As American and Russian players chased after the ball, the crowd spilled onto the floor. Happy Americans, thinking they had won, leaped into the air.

But an Olympic official pushed his way onto the court and waved the crowd back. The game wasn't over yet. Although the clock showed one second remaining, he ordered it to be reset at three seconds. A furious Hank Iba began to argue with the official, but the clock was reset at three seconds. When play resumed, the Russians would again have the ball out of bounds.

The Russians anchored a 6-foot-8 forward, Aleksander Belov, near their basket. Hank Iba figured that the Russians would hurl a long pass to Belov. The clock would not start ticking until Belov touched the ball, so he would have three full seconds to try to sink a basket. Iba told two of his players to stand on each side of Belov and try to intercept or deflect the pass.

The whistle blew, and the game continued. Iba had guessed correctly. A Russian lofted a long pass to Belov at the other end of the court. Belov leaped to catch it —and so did the two Americans. The three players collided. Arms and legs tangled, the Americans crashed to the floor. Belov grabbed the ball, pivoted, and dropped in a shot just as the buzzer sounded for the final time. Immediately the arena was filled with the sounds of happy Russians and enraged Americans. The Russians had won, 51–50 —or had they?

The Americans claimed that the last three seconds should never have been replayed and filed a written protest to that effect. Olympic officials upheld the Russians' victory. They said that the Russians had tried to call a time-out after Collins's second free throw, and that's why the clock was set back three seconds. Later, the Russians stood high on the victory stand and received the first basketball gold medal to be awarded to anyone but an American.

America's loss in the Olympics was inevitable. By 1972 almost every nation had good players. Teams from Spain, Italy, France, and many other countries competed annually for a European basketball championship. Teams from Japan and the Philippines had their own competitions. In the 80 years since Jim Naismith's students had brought the game to kids around the globe, basketball had become second only to soccer as the world's most popular team sport. America's defeat in the Olympics was proof positive that America's Game had become the World's Game.

Thinking they've won the Olympic gold medal, happy Americans begin their celebration (left). Seconds later (right) they learn the bad news: the Russians have won.

35

Call the Doctor

At the start of the 1973–74 season, NBA and ABA fans were still arguing about the relative merits of their league. Some NBA fans insisted there was no comparison: next to their own 27-year-old league, the ABA was just a young upstart. But even the most avid NBA fans had to admit that the new league had just about the most exciting player in all of pro basketball. His name was Julius Erving, but everyone called him Dr. J.

Julius Erving was a man of a thousand moves—and no two, it seemed, were alike. The 6-foot-6 forward leaped higher than most seven-footers, and he hovered in the air like a helicopter. Time after time, he tossed in shots that left even hardened pros gasping. "Maybe three times a game," said a teammate, "he'll do something to blow my mind and leave the guys on the bench looking at each other and shaking their heads."

"When I first saw him," another teammate recalled, "I thought: 'Oh-oh, just another showboat.' But then you see that he does more than lead the team in scoring. He's our best shot blocker. He's our best ball stealer. He's our best passer. He's our best rebounder. He uses all the things he can do with the marvelous hinged body of his to the best advantage of the team."

In 1973, after two whirlwind seasons with the ABA's Virginia Squires, the high-scoring Dr. J. was acquired by the New York Nets for a million dollars. Then Net owner Ray Boe signed Dr. J. to a $2.5 million contract for eight years. "And he'll be worth every penny," Boe predicted.

Dr. J. joined a Net team that had won only 30 of 84 games during the previous season. The team was the youngest in pro basketball, and the average age of the players was only 22. (Like Dr. J., most of the Nets had quit college to pocket some of the huge sums of money being thrown around by the warring leagues.)

Even with Dr. J. in the line-up, the Nets were given little chance to win the 1973–74 ABA championship. The defending champions, the Indiana Pacers, had won the title two years in a row. They seemed likely to make it three straight. The only other team that seemed to have a crack at the title was the Kentucky Colonels. The Colonels had a great shot-blocking center, 7-foot-2 Artis Gilmore, and such high-scoring stars as Dan Issel and Lou Dampier.

When the season began, however, the Nets surprised everyone by getting off to a fast start. And they kept up their winning pace for the rest of the season. Dr. J. led the league in scoring, averaging 27 points a game. Two other Nets, center Billy Paultz and forward Larry Kenon, pitched in another 30 points per game between them.

"Dr. J. could score forty or fifty points a night," said Net coach Kevin Loughery. "But he only wants to score twenty-five or so. He knows that a team wins with a balanced offense—four or five guys scoring fifteen to thirty points a game, not one man scoring fifty points while the other four stand around and watch."

New York's balanced offense shot them into first place in the ABA East. And with Dr. J. leading the fast-break, the young Nets outran the older and slower Virginia Squires in the opening round of the playoffs.

After erasing the Squires in five games, the Nets took on the Kentucky Colonels for

Julius Erving flies to the hoop for one of his favorite shots—the slam dunk.

the Eastern championship. Again Dr. J. led the way. In one game the score was tied and only a few seconds remained. Julius caught a pass at the foul circle. Immediately two Colonels sandwiched him between them. Clutching the ball in his right hand, Dr. J. leaped away from his defenders like a man doing a swan dive. His nose was pointed at the floor. But he let go of the ball with a sharp flick of his wrist. As the final buzzer ripped through the din, the ball dropped into the hoop for the game-winning goal.

The Nets swept by the Colonels in four games to win the Eastern title. Meanwhile, in the West, the once-mighty Pacers were upset by the Utah Stars. Then the Stars and the Nets went on to the finals.

In one game, most of the Net shooters

JULIUS ERVING ■close-up■

"As a kid, I played a lot of one on none," Julius Erving once said, recalling his early childhood. In the 1950s Julius played alone on a playground in Roosevelt, Long Island, a New York suburb. From early in the morning to late at night Julius heaved jump shots at the hoop. Most of those shots hit the rim and bounced away.

Julius tried out for his high school team. He was still a poor jump shooter. But he was 6-foot-3 and could leap to incredible heights for rebounds. In his sophomore and junior years he was a second-string forward. "Practice your moves around the hoop," his coach told him. "If you can shake off your man, you can catch a pass and put in lay-ups. You'll get the same points that other guys get with long jump shots."

By his senior year the springy-legged Julius could jump higher than 6-foot-9 centers. And he could swoop like a roller coaster toward the hoop. "I can float and change direction easily in the air better than most players," he once said. "It is that freedom of motion that separates me from the others."

One of Julius's high school friends called himself "The Professor." Julius began to call himself "The Doctor." The Doctor's leaps around the hoop drew college scouts to Roosevelt. Julius, now 6-foot-6, accepted an offer from the University of Massachusetts.

In his first varsity season, Julius averaged 20 rebounds and 26 points a game. His junior year was more of the same. He averaged 19 rebounds (tops in the nation) and 27 points. There are no statistics for Erving's senior year in college (1971–72). By then he was playing in the pros. The ABA Virginia Squires had signed him for one million dollars.

As a rookie with the Squires, Julius was a high-scoring sensation. A teammate, Willie Sojourner, began to call him Dr. J. The Atlanta Hawks tried to lure Dr. J. to the NBA with an offer of a million-and-a-half dollars. Dr. J. was ready to go. But the Squires appealed to a judge, and the judge ordered Dr. J. to stay in Virginia. Dr. J. obeyed, and the next season he led the ABA in scoring with 32 points a game. Then New York Net owner Ray Boe ended the wrangling by purchasing the rights to Dr. J.

Erving's leaps, swoops, and stuffs seemed to make the young Nets play with extra dash and flair. "It's all psychological," Dr. J. explained after the Nets won the 1974 ABA title. "If we're down a few points and I'm fast-breaking toward the hoop, I'll sometimes decide that the time has come to get freaky. It gets the crowd up and our team up and it gets me up. Because of the excitement we'll often start to defend better, to make good plays, and to pull ahead."

In one game Dr. J. leaped high to toss a court-length pass to a teammate breaking for the hoop. An opponent rose on his right to block the pass. Still in midair, Dr. J. spun like a top. And as he whirled, he flashed the ball from his right hand to his left. Only then did he zing the ball to his teammate, who put in an easy lay-up.

After the game a reporter said to Dr. J., "I never saw anyone do something like that."

Dr. J. looked up at the reporter and coolly replied, "It was the only way I was able to get the job done."

132

Kentucky's Dan Issel lays in a two-pointer during the 1974 ABA playoffs against the Nets.

went cold. So Dr. J. went on a scoring spree and dashed in 47 points. But in the rest of the games he scored his usual 25 or 30 points and steered the ball to his teammates for the rest. The Nets won three of the first four games and went into game five needing only one more victory for the championship. That night Dr. J. really moved the ball around, and the Nets' offense couldn't have been more balanced. Julius scored 20 points while Larry Kenon put in 23, Billy Paultz 21, Brian Taylor 19, and John Williamson 15. With a true team effort, the Nets beat the Stars, 111–100, for their first ABA championship.

The following season (1974–75), Dr. J. was the league's second-highest scorer with 27 points a game. The Pacers' George McGinnis topped him with a 29-point average. Although Dr. J. and the Nets had a good year, they were eliminated early in the play-

offs. The Pacers climbed all the way to the finals, where they ran into the Kentucky Colonels. Led by Gilmore, Issel, and Dampier, the Colonels defeated the Pacers to win the 1975 ABA championship.

In the summer of 1975 the ABA lost one of its brightest stars. George McGinnis jumped to the NBA, signing with the Philadelphia 76ers for more than three million dollars for six years—half a million dollars per season. But the ABA gained some new stars, too. David Thompson, an All-America from North Carolina State, signed a contract with the ABA's Denver Nuggets, also for a half million dollars per season. He was the highest-paid rookie in the history of pro basketball. Probably the youngest rookie in pro basketball history was 19-year-old Moses Malone. A 6-foot-11 center, Malone was plucked out of high school by Denver. Instead of playing for a college freshman

133

Super-rookies David Thompson (left) and Moses Malone (right) received huge salaries to join the ABA.

team, he played for the Nuggets—at a salary of more than $250,000 a season.

Old-timers like Nat Holman, who remembered playing for $50 a game, sighed. Even current players were astonished. "There's no way I'm worth three million dollars to play basketball," said George McGinnis. "I used to play it for nothing. This war between the leagues is so stupid."

The costs of the bidding war finally became too much. In 1975-76 two of the ABA teams folded. Then, shortly after the season, the ABA agreed to merge four of its teams with the NBA. The new league had never quite been the equal of the NBA, but in the end its four strongest teams, including Julius Erving's Nets, survived.

36
Women Who Win

Some 12,000 fans settled into their seats on a Saturday afternoon in 1975 for a college double-header at Madison Square Garden. During the years since the point-shaving scandals of the 1950s, attendance at these double-headers had steadily crept upwards in big-city arenas all over the country. Although college basketball games no longer drew the packed houses of the 1930s and '40s, college students and their friends still lined up to see their teams whenever they came to the Garden.

But this crowd was unusual. It was larger than most, but more important, it was com-

Immaculata's Mary Schraff drives to the hoop in a game against Queens College at Madison Square Garden.

posed mainly of women. And with good reason. Before the men of Fairfield University and the University of Massachusetts met in the second game of the doubleheader, the all-women teams from New York's Queens College and Pennsylvania's Immaculata College would compete in the opener.

Women had been playing basketball ever since Jim Naismith invented the game in 1891. But in the early 1900s high school and college officials had decided that basketball was too strenuous for women and come up with a modified version of the game for the "weaker sex." But women didn't like the slower-paced, less exciting game. And by 1970, as feminists campaigned for equal rights, many high school teams and all the college teams went back to playing by men's rules. In fact, college women of the '70s played an even faster game than college men. Women's teams had to shoot within 30 seconds or give up the ball.

In 1972 college women began to play in their own national tournaments. The first Association for Intercollegiate Athletics for Women (AIAW) Tournament was won by Immaculata College. Starring for Immaculata was 5-foot-11 Teresa Shank. "I never would have played girls' basketball in high school if they hadn't changed the rules and let us play like the boys play," she said. "I hated girls' basketball rules."

Starring for a high school team in Philadelphia, Teresa played before crowds of 6,000. And in college she and her Immaculata teammates competed in the huge Maryland University Cole Field House. That game was televised by a TV network, a first for women's basketball.

In 1973 Teresa and her teammates won their second AIAW championship in a row, and in 1974 they made it three straight. The Immaculata players began to call themselves "the UCLA of the East." The Mighty Macs, as the team was also called, won 35 straight games. In 1974, however, their

winning streak was snapped by Queens College.

Now, here at the Garden, a year after that upset, Queens and Immaculata were meeting for a rematch. "We've been the best a long while," said Immaculata guard Mary Schraff. "But we can't say we're the best if Queens beats us again."

Immaculata proved it was still number one by defeating Queens, 65–61. Mary Schraff led the way with 12 points and 9 rebounds. "I wasn't concerned about scoring," she said after the game. "I was more concerned about finding the open woman, and getting to the boards." "It was a rough game," added a Queens forward, showing her bruises to a reporter. "I'm black and blue all over."

The 1975 AIAW tournament pitted Immaculata against Delta State (Mississippi) College, an exciting match-up. Immaculata was hoping to win its fourth straight title, and Delta was looking to cap off an undefeated (28–0) regular season with the championship. There could be only one winner, however, and that turned out to be Delta State. With 6-foot-3 center Lusia Harris chipping in 32 points, Delta outscored Immaculata, 90–81.

The Delta women kept right on winning in 1975–76. They stretched their winning streak to 51 games—a record for women's college basketball—before bowing to their rivals from Immaculata late in the season. But Delta got revenge in the '76 AIAW finals, defending its championship with a 69–64 victory over the Mighty Macs.

The best of all women's basketball teams in the 1970s, however, was probably the All-American Red Heads. Organized in the 1930s as a touring pro team, the Red Heads were still hopping around the country forty years later. Of course, the line-up had changed over the years. But the team was as successful as ever. Playing against men's teams in the cities and towns they visited, the Red Heads racked up a 188–13 record in 1974. The Red Heads claimed they could beat many men's college teams—a challenge that was never accepted.

In 11 years with the Red Heads, sharp-shooting Jolene Ammons put in more than 21,000 points—a record for women players.

The Basketball Hall of Fame, in Springfield, Massachusetts, asked the 5-foot-9 Red Head to donate her jersey so it could be displayed next to the jersey of the highest-scoring man in basketball—Wilt Chamberlain, who had put in more than 31,000 points as a pro.

Delta State's Lusia Harris (45) outleaps Immaculata's Sandy Miller for the center tap.

The first woman in NCAA history to compete in a men's varsity game, Cyndi Meserve of Pratt tries to grab a loose ball away from her rivals.

Another Red Head, Karen Logan, almost made the U.S. Olympic team as a 400-meter runner. She was also a junior tennis champion. She began to play basketball in her teens, and by 1975 she was averaging 24 points a game as a Red Head. "We are the best women's basketball team ever," she told people.

As more and more women began to play basketball, however, there were bound to be other teams to challenge that claim. In 1975 *Sports Illustrated* reported that "basketball now ranks as the most popular sport among high school girls, and breakthroughs are being made almost every day at the collegiate level."

One big breakthrough came later that year when 19-year-old Cyndi Meserve became the first woman to play against men in an NCAA basketball game. A 5-foot-8 guard for New York's Pratt Institute, Cyndi played only a few minutes in her first game and didn't score. But in another game she dropped in a pair of free throws. More important, she proved that college women could play against college men.

The biggest breakthrough for women players all over the world, however, came in the summer of 1976 at Montreal. For the first time ever, women's basketball teams from all over the world competed in the Olympic Games.

37

Champions and Challengers

As the 1970–71 season got under way, the New York Knicks were the defending champions of the National Basketball Association. The young Knicks dreamed of lording it over the NBA for many years to come—just as the Celtics had reigned during the 1950s and '60s. But their dreams faded fast. For the next six seasons no team would win the championship two years in a row.

The Milwaukee Bucks were the team to beat for the 1971 NBA title. The Bucks had just acquired Oscar Robertson from the Cincinnati Royals. The Bucks had paid $250,000 to sign the Big O—and they considered it money well spent. Robertson, the highest-scoring guard of all time, would be joining another great shooter, Kareem Abdul-Jabbar, on the Bucks. The previous season Kareem had led Milwaukee in scoring with 28 points a game. Now with Kareem and Oscar, the Bucks had what many considered the best big man and the best little man in basketball.

Kareem and Oscar led the Bucks to a 66–16 record in 1970–71. In one stretch Milwaukee won 20 games in a row. But the Bucks weren't shoo-ins for the NBA championship. During the regular season they had played the Knicks five times—and come out on top just once. If the Bucks met the Knicks in the playoff finals, many people expected the Knicks to win.

The Knicks never got that far, however. They were eliminated in the opening round of the playoffs by the Baltimore Bullets. But the Bucks swept by the San Francisco Warriors and the Chicago Bulls to win the Western championship. And in the finals, they wiped out the Bullets to win the 1971 championship.

By 1971–72 the Big O was 34 years old and having trouble with his legs. Kareem Abdul-Jabbar topped the league in scoring for the second-straight year. But even with Kareem, the Bucks couldn't match the scoring of the Los Angeles Lakers. With Wilt Chamberlain, Jerry West, Gail Goodrich, and Jim McMillian pouring in points, the Lakers reeled off 33 straight victories—the longest winning streak by any big-league pro team in history. And they finished the season with the best NBA record ever—69 victories against only 13 losses.

The Lakers breezed through the early playoff rounds and made it to the finals—their ninth in the past 14 seasons. In each one of those previous finals, the Lakers had fallen short of the championship. To win it this year, they'd have to get past the Knicks. In the first game of the series, however, the Knicks' firing squad outshot the Lakers, 114–92. "Same old story," Laker fans grumbled as they left the Los Angeles Forum. "The Lakers can't win the big games."

As if to prove the fans wrong, the Lakers bounced right back and won the next three games. In one game Chamberlain broke his wrist. But Wilt just taped the wrist and came out to play in the fifth game. If the Lakers won now, they would finally have a championship. And Wilt was determined to see that they did. That night he pulled down 29 rebounds, and the Lakers beat the Knicks, 114–100.

The next season (1972–73), the Knicks welcomed back their burly captain, Willis Reed, who had sat out much of the previous season with aching knees. A high scorer, Reed was also the shot blocker that the

Milwaukee's Kareem Abdul-Jabbar stuffs the ball into the hoop despite the defensive efforts of Bullet Wes Unseld.

Knicks needed for their gambling team defense.

Reed helped make the Knicks the best defensive team in the league. In the 1973 finals a great defense (the Knicks) met a great offense (the Lakers), and the defense triumphed. It took the Knicks only five games to knock the Lakers off the NBA throne. For the second time in four years, the Knicks were champs.

In the 1973–74 season, however, Reed hobbled back to the sidelines on aching legs. And many of the other Knicks—Dave De-Busschere, Earl "The Pearl" Monroe, Dick Barnett, and Jerry Lucas—were slowed down by age or injury. A young Celtic team ran by the Knicks to win the Eastern championship, then advanced to the finals against the giant Kareem and the Bucks.

There were few familiar faces on this 1974 Celtic team. Only John Havlicek and sub Don Nelson remained from the Celtic dynasty of the 1960s. A relative newcomer to the line-up was Dave Cowens, now in his fourth season with Boston. A 6-foot-8 center, he played the game with a fiery intensity that matched his red hair. Voted the league's Most Valuable Player in 1973, the young superstar hadn't even reached his peak yet. "He is the new kind of center. Strong as a Chamberlain but as quick as a Cousy," said Tommy Heinsohn, who was now the coach of his old team.

But as the Celtics prepared to challenge the Bucks in the finals, many fans feared that even Cowens wouldn't be able to contain Milwaukee's Kareem Abdul-Jabbar.

"We'll give you no help in guarding Abdul-Jabbar," Heinsohn told Cowens. "Try to run in circles around him so the Bucks can't get the ball to him as often as they would like. If you can hold Jabbar to thirty or thirty-five points, our defense should be able to limit the scoring of Oscar Robertson and the other Bucks and we can win."

In the first game Kareem looped in 35

Knicks Jerry Lucas (32) and Dave DeBus-schere battle Laker Jim McMillian for possession of the ball, but it's big Wilt (hidden) who finally gets his hand on it.

points. But the Boston defenders refused to let any other Buck score more than ten. Boston won, 98–93. In the second game, however, the Bucks' Bob Dandridge broke loose for 24 points, Kareem put in 36, and the Bucks won, 105–96.

Boston center Dave Cowens bats a rebound away from Milwaukee's Bob Dandridge during the 1974 NBA finals.

The teams battled to a seventh game, which was played in Milwaukee. There Cowens collected 28 points and held Abdul-Jabbar to 26. And no other Buck scored more than 15. The fast-breaking Celtics raced to a 102–87 triumph. Once more the Celtics had won a seventh game. Once more they stood atop the NBA.

In 1974–75, however, the Celtics lost

their crown to the most unlikely challengers. Before the season began, the Golden State Warriors (the team was now playing in Oakland and had a new name) were picked to finish as low as fifth in the five-team NBA Pacific Division. (By now the league had expanded to 17 teams and was divided into four divisions.) The Warriors had only one bona fide star—Rick Barry. After bouncing around the ABA for several seasons, he'd come back to the NBA in 1972 and was averaging close to 30 points a game for the Warriors.

The Warriors' center, 6-foot-9 Cliff Ray, had put in only nine points a game the previous season. One guard, Butch Beard, had been traded by three teams in four years. The other guard, Charley Johnson, scored fewer than six points a game. Coach Al Attles had to start 6-foot-6 Keith Wilkes at forward. Wilkes was only a rookie, but he'd put in plenty of points during his college career at UCLA.

In desperation, Attles finally decided to give all 12 of his players the maximum amount of playing time. By making the most of his bench, he'd always have a new wave of fresh players ready for action. Hopefully, they'd be able to run by tired opponents to outscore them. Instead of one player scoring 20 points a game, he thought he might come up with two who could score 10 each.

And that's just about the way it worked out. Rick Barry had another super season and put in 30 points a game. The other eleven players pitched in so many points that the Warriors averaged 108 per game—the most in the NBA.

The Warriors won their division title. And in the playoffs they climbed to the finals against the Washington (formerly, Baltimore) Bullets. The Bullets' number one scorer was Elvin Hayes, the former All-America from Houston. No one expected the Warriors to get past the Bullets—no one but Coach Attles, that is. "Stop Hayes and we've got a chance," Attles told his team.

In the first game Attles raided his bench for a steady stream of fresh players to guard the Big E. But Hayes shook off the defenders and crammed in 29 points. The Warriors came from behind in the second half, however, as subs Phil Smith and Charlie Dudley teamed up to contribute points. The Warriors won, 101–95.

"Our bench won it for us," exulted Attles.

Golden State rookie Keith Wilkes has his eye on the basket during the 1975 championships.

"But that's nothing new. They've done it all year."

The Warriors kept doing it, too. They won the next game, and the next, and most incredibly, the one after that. In four straight games, the underdog Warriors swept the series to win the 1975 NBA championship.

143

Rick Barry clears a path through Bullets Elvin Hayes and Kevin Porter.

Rick Barry summed up the significance of the Warrior victory for anyone who wants to win a basketball championship.

"I used to be selfish," he said, "and think I could win a game pretty much all by myself. But this year I learned you can win if you've got five starters and a benchload of players who care about each other and are dedicated to one thing only—winning."

But only a year later Rick Barry was disgusted with his team. In the semi-final round of the 1976 playoffs, the champion Warriors were upset in seven games by the Phoenix Suns, who had been last in their division only a few months earlier. "The Suns made us look like a bunch of rookies," Rick growled.

Once more, the NBA king was dead. The new king would be either the Suns—a team without a single All-Pro player—or the Boston Celtics, who had been hobbled by injuries most of the year. Veterans John Havlicek and Dave Cowens were still the Celts' big guns, but two shooting guards, Jo Jo White and Charlie Scott, had kept Boston in the race.

The Celtics won the first two games of the finals, but the Suns won the next two. The fifth game, played before the screaming fans of Boston, was one of the great playoff contests in history.

In the closing moments of regulation time, the teams were tied 95–95. Each team got a free throw that could have won the game, and while the fans held their breaths, each team missed.

The first overtime ended with the score still tied. The exhausted players panted into a second overtime. With five seconds left, Phoenix led, 110–109. Then the old reliable, John Havlicek, who had played the whole series with an injured foot, tossed in an off-balance shot. Boston led, 111–110, with no time showing on the clock. Delirious Boston fans swarmed onto the court.

Officials signaled that a second remained. After the floor was cleared, the Suns called time-out to move the ball to midcourt. But they had no time-outs left. The Celts, awarded a free throw, scored to lead, 112–110.

The Suns' Garfield Heard took the pass from out of bounds and threw a "prayer" shot at the basket. It swished through the nets and the game was tied once again! The fans went back to their seats, hardly believing that a third overtime would be needed.

Jo Jo White sank six points for the Celtics. The Suns came back, but not fast enough. When the clock ran out, Boston led 128–126. The loss killed the Suns' spirit, and the Celtics won the 6th game and their 13th championship in 20 years.

The winning general manager, Red Auerbach, had watched pro basketball grow from its earliest years. The coach, Tom Heinsohn, had been a Celtic rookie the year the team won its first championship. And John Havlicek, who had contributed to a Boston championship in 1963, was still a mainstay 13 years later.

How had the Celtics won in 1976 against the increasingly stiff competition in the NBA? John Havlicek grinned and said, "In Boston we call it Celtic Pride."

Veteran Celtic John Havlicek keeps the ball under heavy pressure from Phoenix in the 1976 playoffs.

38
Big and Little Giants

Basketball's first great stars were small, quick players—Nat Holman, Hank Luisetti, and Bob Cousy. Then the big men took over. Towering centers such as George Mikan, Bill Russell, and Wilt Chamberlain overshadowed their shorter rivals. Some fans began to complain that basketball was a game for giants only.

But today's new stars come in every size and shape. Flashy little guards such as "Pistol" Pete Maravich and "Tiny" Nate Archibald and bulky centers such as Elvin Hayes and Bob McAdoo all make unique contributions to their teams.

Pete Maravich . . .

. . . Nate Archibald . . .

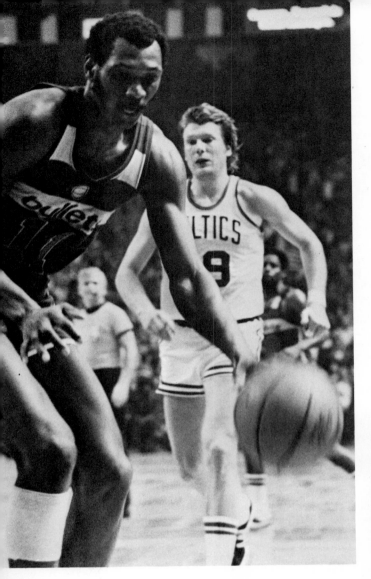

be quick, smooth, and agile. Elvin Hayes and Bob McAdoo (both 6-foot-9) are all of that and more. Perennial scoring leaders, they float in jumpers from outside and streak to the hoop with an ease that belies their great height. And, of course, they get more than their share of dunk shots.

"Today's great centers score like little guards," said one coach. "And today's little guards score like big centers." Today's superstars—from Tiny Nate to the Big E—are proof positive that basketball is a game for everyone. And that's just what Dr. Naismith had in mind when he invented the game.

. . . and Bob McAdoo.

. . . Elvin Hayes . . .

In three record-breaking seasons at Louisiana State University, Maravich led the nation's collegians in scoring. And later, as an NBA superstar, he dropped in 27 points a game during the 1973–74 season to equal the average that year of 7-foot-2 center Kareem Abdul-Jabbar.

Nate Archibald, barely six feet tall, did even better in 1972–73. He topped Kareem —and everyone else in the NBA—by whistling in almost 35 points a game. A slick playmaker, Tiny also earned the number one spot in the assists column that year. (It was the first time in NBA history that one player led the league in both departments.)

To keep up with such speedsters as Maravich and Archibald, today's big men must

Index

Page numbers in italics refer to photographs.

149